THE SAGA OF THE AMERICAN SOUL

Richard E. Wentz

UNIVERSITY
PRESS OF
AMERICA

For Yvonne

TABLE OF CONTENTS

PREFACE

This book is a venture into canyon country. There is always the danger of falling rocks, rushing waters, ambush, falling, or getting lost. But one chances it, because there is a need --perhaps there is the seductive lure of the forbidden, the difficult and the exotic. This is not to make some extravagant claim for the book itself. I have no delusions about what is found within these covers. When I began the writing, I was filled with great visions of what I wished to accomplish. But like all else I have sought to do, this work falls short of the glory I had contemplated. I accept that fate.

What follows is neither history nor theology, neither criticism nor systematic argument. What I set out to do is described in the first chapter, and I will not reproduce an explanation here. I suppose, if I were to attempt any classification, telling what kind of book this is, I would call it a religiosophy of the American experience. That is to say, my assumption is that there is wisdom and insight (sophos) about the meaningful character of existence (religio) to be derived from an understanding of American history. But more than that, such religiosophical truth is desperately needed by Americans searching for ways to relate their particularity responsibly to existence in a global and cosmic world.

Because I believe that the uniqueness of the American experience need not breed imperialism, I must try to describe why this is so. Because I believe that human beings always exist meaningfully and actively in response to symbols which motivate thought and imagination, I wish to write about the Americanness of some symbols which are essential to human dignity and survival. I subscribe to no particular theory of symbolization or historical interpretation. Therefore, I have avoided formal methodological discussion. People think and act and imagine, not by way of theory, but as a result of historical interaction and response. The degree of creative awareness of that fact determines the

vii

course of responsible existence. This book is an
attempt at the celebration of that truth.

To speak of America is to tell a story,
a cultural story--what I believe is a saga. No
story is ever told without the use of images. It
is on a few of the basic images of the American
story that I wish to reflect in these pages. There
are other images, other symbols, but one must
choose. I have chosen these particular images
because, were I to tell the saga itself, I could
not get on with it, without these images.

There is no formal conclusion to the
chapters that follow. The conclusion is contained
in each chapter and is confined to none because
"the saga of the American soul" must be continuing
and dynamic. The book may not be easy going for
some. For others, there may be the frustration of
unconsummated desire. If there are those who find
my ideas helpful and stimulating, my work is justified and my purposes achieved. To others I must
apologize for my presumption.

I acknowledge a Faculty Grant-in-Aid from
Arizona State University which provided opportunity
for reflection and writing on this project while I
was dutifully immersed in research on other matters.
My wife and three daughters suffered my fits of
agony and endured my preachments on the subject.
The reader will probably be able to discern the
influence of many scholars and authors, but I will
acknowledge homage to no one in order to protect
such potential recipients from dubious honors. To
the reading of American religious history, to a
fascination with the history of religions, to a
certain speculative twist of mind--to these I lift
my acknowledgments. But most of all, to those
secretaries who translated my hieroglyphics into
typescript, I acknowledge my greatest debt; and
especially to Marilyn Krauskopf for producing the
final copy.

Richard E. Wentz

CHAPTER I

DISCOVERING THE AMERICAN SAGA

I have stood with Christopher Columbus and John Winthrop, on board ships whose mission had to do with extending the human horizon beyond the tear-stained shores of Iberia and Essex. As a political being I understood that power comes from knowing what others only dimly perceive, from possessing what others long for. As a child of the Church, I knew that there would be rejoicing "in heaven in the prospect of the salvation of souls of so many nations hitherto lost." I have been a son of Christendom, have sailed and marched and prayed with Jesuit fathers on the banks of the Colorado River. I can tread the wistful soil of Antietam and Gettysburg, and feel the loneliness of battle among a hundred cousins. And in the stillness there is a "malice toward none; with charity for all" that washes the wounds of a nation still beathed in injustice. I have even felt the song vibrate from my soul to the whip in my hand: "Oh, Freedom! Freedom over me! Before I'd be a slave, I'd be buried in my grave and go home to my Lord and be free!" For I know that many ships have made their way to the shores of America. Some have had passengers whose only hope was the sale of their labor in this unseen Paradise where the stains of deprivation and persecution would be cleansed. But there were "goodly vessels" whose ironic "laugh at all disaster" was wrenched from the swollen throats of oarsmen chained to duty, and unwilling pilgrims whose shackled feet lay bare in stinking holds.

Somehow, there are times when I can even recall the sacramental moment of a prehistoric migration from Asian waters along the sweep of the Arctic Circle, through currents that swirl from the heart of the universe, bringing me finally to Oraibi in the land of the Hopi, or perhaps to another sacred center known only to my fathers and mothers in the civilized Confederacy of the Iroquois.

"No people can be bound to acknowledge

1

and adore the Invisible Hand which conducts the
affairs of man more than those of the United States.
Every step by which we have advanced to the character of an independent nation seems to have been
distinguished by some token of providential agency
..." Those are George Washington's words at his
first inauguration. They are my words in whatever
language I can utter them, fashioned into the
script by hands of many colors. They are part of
our common and continuing drama, played out in the
smaller scenes of tribes and tongues, pressing on
to larger destiny. And in our varied individual
episodes, we cling to a universal dream, expressed
by John F. Kennedy: "We observe today...a celebration of freedom--symbolizing an end as well as a
beginning--signifying renewal as well as change...
the same revolutionary beliefs for which our
forebears fought are still at issue around the
globe--the belief that the rights of man come not
from the generosity of the state but from the hand
of God."

I.

        America is more than geography. It is a
saga to be discovered. And saga is a demonstration
of the fact that life is participation in a narrative. We are the participants in a saga which
bears the very meaning of human existence in its
unfolding account. America is the faith and hope
of many who have never touched its shores.
America is the actualization of the fact that the
"last, best hope of earth" is discovered by those
who allow their private visions to lead them to
distant shores where human perception is always
more universal than our petty comprehension
acknowledges.

        Some of the meaning of what I am trying
to interpret first came to me in a series of
unusual associations after I moved to Arizona in
the summer of 1972. I had never visited the South-
west before, had never seen the desert. I had been
a lifelong Pennsylvanian, one whose German ancestry
had known that deep-rooted effect of forest and

mountain upon the human spirit. Reality, for me, had been very much dependent upon that setting, but I had never thought about its significance. What is true and beautiful had acquired intelligibility in the milieu of *Wald und Berg*. The confidence and loyalty in which my life had been directed were uniquely formed by those contours.

I became aware of all this for the first time when I began the descent by car from Flagstaff in the north of Arizona to the great Phoenix in the Valle del Sol. There was a gradual vanishing of familiar landmarks. The pine-tipped skyline with its verdant fullness gave way to a flushing of reds and browns. Soon the vegetation began to change and I saw those unique children of the Arizona desert, the saguaro cacti. They coolly waved their husky arms in the midst of heightening temperatures. The effect on me was radical and unexpected. It was one of the few times in my life that I was strongly aware of the numinous. The experience was *mysterium fascinans, mysterium tremendum*. The beauty of the desert for someone who has never seen it is overwhelming, and I'm told by some natives that it's a sensibility that never disappears. The sensation is like that of Odysseus, being drawn to the Isle of Circe. It is a seduction with the promise of destruction in its siren call. I began to understand why it is that so many people die in the desert. (I used to wonder why they went there in the first place.) For months after my first encounter with the Arizona desert I lived with a profound sense of the precariousness of existence. As Mircea Eliade has shown us, the desert is the chaos at the edge of victorious existence. But here in this valley human civilization has arranged its cosmos around a sacred center right in the midst of the desert. Long before the coming of Europeans, the Hohokam had developed a high culture in the drainages of the Salt River.

Then one day I stood in my backyard, overlooking the tops of citrus trees, date palms, and Aleppo pines. I heard a familiar voice, but at first I paid no attention to it. My consciousness failed to register those notes until a later

3

time when I sat reading, doing some research into
the folk traditions of early Pennsylvania. In that
literature I began to notice the image of the
turtledove. There she was, in the art and in the
mystical life of my forebears. Then I *remembered*
her voice from atop the wall at my new home in the
desert.

>   The flowers appear on the earth,
>   The time of singing has come,
>   And the voice of the turtledove
>   Is here in our land.
>   (Song of Songs 2:12)

It was apposite. I was conscious of a promise and
trust that had been offered me in the midst of the
experience of the precarious. The sensation of
chaos is somehow essential to a knowledge of the
basic power of meaning that is constantly in
immediate relationship to us. There is always the
gentle reminder of the sacred trust of existence.
It must have been that way for Columbus, when,
precariously listing off the coast of San
Salvadore (Holy Savior), he entered these words in
the log book: "Sunday, September 23rd. Sailed
N.W. and N.W. by N. and at times W. nearly twenty-
two leagues. Saw a turtle dove..." The awareness
of such a sign confronts us with the presence of
the undergirding and sustaining power of meaning
that is always available to us.

        Since I have used the term "apposite,"
it may be well to attempt an explanation of its
meaning at this point. It is my contention that
life itself is appositional; that it is more profound, significant, and useful to understand it in
that manner than to engage in various forms of
abstract reasoning about such things as essence
versus existence, being versus becoming, or ideal
versus real. To discover the appositional is to
understand that life is always relational, that we
are always set in relationship to a More Than that
offers itself to us in meaning and power. Thus,
when I read a poem or utter a prayer, I may
suddenly discover that I have found satisfaction
and courage for living, even though I have acquired

no definite *explanations* for anything. I have
simply demonstrated the constancy of the truth that
reality is appositional.

Take, for example, the grammatical use of
the word "apposite." There are two nuances of
meaning. Something is apposite, when "one sub-
stantive is placed beside another" thereby explaining it. And so, I will say, "Tammy, my faithful
collie." The word "Tammy" is meaningless without
the appositional reference. There is another shade
of meaning, suggesting a biological significance--
the growth or increase of one thing by the juxta-
position of another. From these two definitions,
we can describe reality itself as appositional.
There is no reality that is not appositional.
Meaning and growth are always derived from the
immediacy of relational characteristics that share
themselves with us. Thus, I am never severed or
suspended from such apposition--not even in
thought. And when I especially discover that words
like

> The flowers appear on the earth,
> The time of singing has come,
> And the voice of the turtledove
> Is here in our land.

are apposite, then I am simply become sensible of
what is constantly true. To discover that something is appropriate, relevant, or pertinent is to
verify the fact that reality itself is an offering
of the power of meaning.

Now, it is my conviction that the truth
of the appositional character of reality is most
aptly expressed in metaphor, that dramatic images
are the clearest expression of truth. If life is
appositional, then saga is the best way to understand it and talk about it. The American experience itself is a demonstration of that fact.
It has taken life to be participation and response.
It has had little time for abstract exercises that
do not reflect the fundamental appositional
character of things. As a result we have been
called activist rather than quietist; we have

5

responded to life by action, and we have "reasoned"
in the wake of dreams and images. Unfortunately,
we have been slow to recognize the value of such
response. And as intellectuals we have been
ashamed of it, rather than availing ourselves of
its great new potential.

Our understanding should be involved in
the critical and appreciative awareness of the
actualities of experience, not in abstractions
that are supposedly self-vindicating. For me, it
matters not whether people remember or use the
word "appositional." What it refers to is the
fact that the power of meaning is always present
to us. We do not create ourselves by existential-
ist fiat. What we "decide" when we arrive at the
place of "No Exit" is based on the "voice of the
turtledove," heard from the maples along the river
as well as from the cottonwoods in the shadow of
the butte. There is no way to think of self or of
meaning without reference to the voice that carries
its promise to us. It is with the *awareness* of
that fact that our thoughts must deal. Life is
appositional, which means that it is understood in
terms of transpersonal meanings which are the basis
of growth and knowledge. Something is always
apposite, sharing meaning and identification with
us. There is no other existence. To know that and
to develop our sensitivity to it is to encounter
life in its fullness--as it is. There are only two
other options: one is to attack life with the mind
or with action, seeking to make it fit our specifications; the other is to consider it illusory or
evil, thence to escape it. That life is appositional is vividly portrayed in the American
experience.

Describe America in a way that does no
justice to what it has meant to people and you have
said nothing at all except to discuss topography or
economics. America cannot be understood except as
a saga, and in turn, you and I are deprived of
meaningful existence if we do not become explorers,
pioneers, and settlers in that saga. America began
as a vision that extended the horizons of humankind
beyond suffering, beyond the myopic sight of wise

men and politicians. The images that filled the
American saga from the beginning had to do with
universal meaning. The saga has always been
greater than the ability of individuals or groups
to comprehend. The American saga is global in
scope, perhaps even cosmic; the faith, hope, and
enterprise of the earth have already been
appreciably influenced by it.

II.

Saga is the bearer of a universalizing
truth. "Our freer, but yet far from freed, land,"
wrote Bronson Alcott, "is the asylum if asylum
there be, for the hope of man; and there, if anywhere, is the second Eden to be planted, in which
the divine seed is to bruise the head of Evil and
restore man to his rightful communion with God in
the Paradise of Good." That statement by the
nineteenth century transcendentalist could almost
serve as a creedal testimony, or a recapitulation
of some of the meaningful images that form the
contours of the American saga. Freedom, hope,
Eden, restoration, communion, Paradise--they are
from a storehouse of images that we must examine
once we discover the saga. There is nothing in
Alcott's declaration that could not be uttered in
good faith by any human being. In one sense, it
merely extolls the obvious. Freedom is process,
says Alcott; freedom, he says, must have a setting
--a place, an asylum--in which the hopes of humankind can have a focus and favorable circumstance.
When Alcott speaks of the second Eden, he proclaims the new creation that must enter into the
consciousness and onto the stage of our dealing
with nature and humanity. It is in such an Eden
that evil is recognized for what it is and a new
order of relationship shall be effected. Who
among the world's peoples does not now share some
version of that creed? It may very well be that
there are those for whom the mournful conditions
of existence seem to jeer the tone of Alcott's
words. However, it must be remembered that the
recognition of such tragedy comes from the depth
of the creed itself; and whatever motivates those
who sense injustices is likewise derived from the

7

mystery and meaning that are in the flow of the American saga.

Alcott's statement uses Biblical imagery to make a more universal proclamation, the truth of which is discovered in the American saga. The American experience is a demonstration of the manner in which particular images and truth-claims constantly have their apparent limitations transcended and drawn to a more universal level. Paul Tillich provided us with a means of discerning this process when, in Christianity and the Encounter of the World Religions, he suggested that in the depth of a given religious tradition there is a point where the particularity of the experience is broken and reveals its affinity to more universal truths. I would prefer to say that it is not so much in the *depths* that we experience the break-through as it is on the appositional *horizons* of history. Those are the moments in which the flow of the saga achieves a peak of perception for us--the occasions in which we perceive the manner whereby freedom calls us out of our present frustration and myopia.

America is a demonstration of the fact that life itself is saga, a continuing unfolding of relationships, a Dynamic Flow of events and meanings. In the course of the saga there are times of great creative response to the unfolding, just as there are instances of awkwardness and obstinacy. We can readily assume that sensibility to the saga itself will in great measure determine whether we shall be creative or phlegmatic. Those for whom the American saga is apposite will become persons who know that the mystery and meaning they have encountered in the saga are particularities that have to do with *universal* human potentiality.

III.

Saga is recognition of the beginning and end of history. "The historical significance of America," wrote John Williamson Nevin at the end of the year 1848, "...lies mainly in this, that the substance of life, as it is to be hereafter is *not* yet fixed, but in the process only of general

8

formation; under such conditions and relations as are needed to bring it finally to a character of universal wholeness and completeness...We cannot speak of our American nationality as a settled and given fact, in the same way that we speak of the nationality of England or France." A saga is never settled, its substance never fixed. The American saga serves as the nexus of an unrecorded past and a recorded history. It is the linkage of all of this to a beckoning future.

In the 1956 film, "These Wilder Years," James Cagney plays Steven Bradford, a tycoon in search of an illegitimate son born twenty years previously. During the course of his search he befriends a sixteen year old girl, Suzie, who is a resident in "The Haven," for unwed mothers and their infants. When Suzie has an accident and is hospitalized, she calls for Bradford. She has rejected an operation to care for internal injuries because she sees no reason to live, and would rather have her child born in safety. Cagney (as Bradford) says something to this effect: "Listen, Suzie. You and I are friends, *old* friends. We were friends long before we ever met. Maybe before we were born. And I don't like to lose an old friend. So, you let them take care of you. D'ya hear?" Somethinf of what Cagney meant is illustrated in the American experience. For in our saga two worlds have been linked. There was the primal world that had formed human nature and seen it through many centuries in which we lived side by side with the rest of the orders of nature. We used our intelligence to understand and cooperate with a world from which we had emerged, to which we were still strongly related. We were all creatures together. And that world was still intact through the Christian culture of the Middle Ages. Then there began to emerge another world. It was produced by the disclosure of what seemed to be a powerful autonomous self, rationally supreme, capable of virtually ignoring the first world--the rest of nature, except to use it to create a new world of knowledge and utility. The two worlds diverged and a new history emerged in which there was born the thought that we could leave the first

world, the primal world, that we could make it on
our own.

America was "discovered" in the course of
the divergence of the two worlds. From the dim
recesses of our minds, from the darkest corners of
that first world, came the recollection of a long-
forgotten "Paradise of Good." America was an "old
friend," long before the soles of kings' and
queens' commissioners touched her winsome strands.
But we have been so enamored of the second world
that we have been pilgrims unaware, settlers in
amnesia, with no understanding of that first world
whose verity is only fixed by metaphor. For much
of the past two hundred years of our history we
have tried to exorcise the truth of that first
world. We have pretended that the second world,
spun like threadlets from our spidery reason, was
the total measure of self, America, and world. But
the first world is never left completely. It is
the most fundamental truth of human existence.
Without a recognition of that world we are less
than human and there is no true self-affirmation--
no way of honoring what it means to exist with
meaning and responsibility.

Yet the saga continues. America is
saga, it offers the nexus of continuity from the
first world to the second. It demonstrates the
fact that life begins before its beginning, that
history itself includes the recollection of what is
unrecorded. "Saga," wrote Karl Barth, "arises
distinct from history and in connexion with it--and
woe to the history which lacks this connexion...
[Saga] looks to the point where from the standpoint
of history everything is dark, although it is only
from this point that 'history' can emerge and be
clear...It looks to the hidden depths of time where
time is already time, and indeed genuine time. It
looks in a most literal sense to the 'radical' time
of history. Where saga...is not allowed to speak,
no true picture of history, i.e., no picture of
true history can ever emerge." How profoundly we
need to reflect on what that means for understanding America. We have been engaged in a journey
that has its roots in a time before time, a journey

10

we only dimly comprehend in each moment of its realization. The saga reminds us of our lost intelligence, our mindful presence in that first world from which we all have come, to which we all belong. Our existence is always more than we can fully describe or penetrate, whether it be by our historical or physical sciences. There is intelligence that is prior to the conscious and deliberate use of intelligence; and there is no absolute separation between the intelligence that is before and that which is conscious. We cannot know the intelligence that is prior except in relation to that which has become deliberate. Nor can we function humanly without an awareness of the intelligence that is prior. Every art and science relies upon that truth, but it is the saga that is the bearer of it. Saga presents us with that sense of organic and continuous unity with all that has been and that will be. There is no history, no biography, no philosophy, and no religion or theology that is not first of all saga. Without the origins, roots, and meanings that saga offers us, there is no meaningful existence. And there is no meaningful existence outside of the saga. We have little choice but to come to terms with the American saga.

When the Puritan fathers tried to express the reason for their "errand into the wilderness," they had no recourse but to think of themselves as under a special commission. They were to live a restored existence. What had been distorted among humans and in the workings of nature had to be renewed. They spoke of a Creator and of Creation in relation to their American pilgrimage. Such designations are derived from the character of life as saga. For when we speak of a Creator we acknowledge the darkness, the void, the time that begins before recorded history, before historical history. By such language we profess that life is prior to our participation in it, yet we can some-how "recall" that darkness out of which all has come. And if we speak of creation, we recognize that the continuity of life itself is at all times greater than our individual or collective selfhood. It comes from beyond us, we are in the midst of it

all. It is more than we are or will be. We are
not yet what we shall be.

The Puritans may not have met the test
of the social conscience of twentieth century
intellectuals, but they knew that justice and
mercy were the "two rules whereby wee are to
walke one towards another." And they knew, too,
that such conscience was necessary not "of any
perticular and singular respect to (man) himselfe
but for the *glory of his Creator and the Common
good of the Creature*, Man..." Human existence
requires a social ethic because it flows out of the
dark beginning of a "before-time" that is
constantly with us. And so the saga begins like
the Book of Genesis in the time before historical
time, with a measure of humanity that is more than
the humanity we know historically.

Think of Abraham Lincoln, one of the
greatest interpreters of the American saga. He saw
the meaning-giving nature of the saga; he was
extremely sensitive to the manner in which the saga
was apposite, yet a reflection of time that is
greater than our measure of it. Our founding
fathers, said Lincoln, had a "majestic interpretation of the *Economy of the universe*...They grasped
not only the whole race of man then living, but
they reached forward and seized upon the farthest
posterity." And that is because the Creator's
purposes are both prior to, and flowing within
creation itself. "'One generation passeth away,
and another generation cometh, but the earth
abideth forever,'" said Lincoln, "It is of the
first importance to duly consider, and estimate,
this ever-enduring part."

When I made my journey from the familiar
temples of *Wald und Berg*, to settle twenty-four
hundred miles away in the Valley of the Sun, in
Arizona, I made a decision much against the advice
of some Pennsylvania friends. They told me that
such a move is best made by selling most home
furnishings, then buying everything new after
arriving at the new location. Instead we brought
pieces of furniture and houseware that had been in

12

our families for years. We moved antique Pennsylvania farm items, whose only real value is that I
had repaired and refinished them myself years
previously. Why did we do this? It was an affair
of bringing our roots. It was out of need for a
familiar and secure setting in a strange land.
But it was more. It was deference to the
character of selfhood as being somehow immersed in
a story that is of the earth and its people, that
reaches back into dimmer beginnings. I heard the
voice of the turtledove in this strange land, and
it was a sign of the nurture of creation itself.
And somehow, I've begun to understand the native
Americans. They knew Creation, too; they know that
life is saga. The ancestors of some of them came
up from the lowest womb of the Earth, womb by womb,
called up out of the darkness, led by the twin gods.
And in their emergence, those ancestors were
changed from primitive creatures into human form.
What an amazing insight into reality! The American
saga includes that insight. It includes also a
knowledge like that of the Hopi, that we have come
from many directions; and the flashing visions of
the spirit world wind their way in procession from
the many corners of the earth, from the dark times
when sight was incapable of record or recognition.
How can I ever claim to be human again, and not
know that the hidden depths of time are part of me,
that the root time of history is part of this
moment and the next?

IV.

Saga is the bearer of personal and social
identity. Who can exist without memory or hope?
They are the heart of identity. Yet such qualities
are not contrived by us; we do not construct them.
If I attempt to fabricate a memory, I exist with
false credentials--perhaps create a fiction that
makes my world illusory or distorts my relation to
my fellow humans. Fictions of memory are proclama-
tions of madmen. Yet just as surely it is a form
of madness, of disorientation, not to have memory.
What is memory but a recapitulation of your episodes, your story within the saga? And the two
levels are so intertwined that it is virtually

13

impossible to say whether my own role must be
remembered first, or whether it is the saga that
assumes priority. Does it really matter? If I
have no memory, I do not know who I am. And if my
memory returns, it probably begins with the
association of some event or person washing across
the water of Lethe. And as my memory collects it
will be more important for me to recall that I am a
resident of Mesa, Arizona, than that I am some
"inner self" with great untapped potential. All of
which means that human identity itself is in great
part the historical discovery of the saga.

        My memory of the whole of the American
saga and my own role in it is the ground of my
identity. To attempt to escape that fact is to
live as an amnesiac, or as an ascetic who rejects
as illusory the very foundation for all thought and
activity. It should also be said that whatever
other kind of reality there may be, the same will
be true of it. If, for example, we posit some form
of "life beyond death," it will also be relational,
not absorption into some ethereal blur of nothing-
ness; or blending into some grotesque mixed and
melted pot of somethingness. Where there is meaning, it is always in terms of my consciousness of
power and sensibility *coming* to me, and sharing
themselves with me. That is what apposition means.
That is what makes it possible to say a prayer or
hear a poem, to be touched by another, and to know
"that everything is alright." C. S. Lewis finds
the truth of this in a brief exchange in the
writings of George MacDonald:

                "You have tasted of death now,"
                    said the Old Man. "Is it
                    good?"
                "Is it good," said Mossy, "It
                    is better than life."
                "No," said the Old Man. "It
                    is only more life."

That is the rule of things--"more life." It is
what makes meaning possible. It is evidence of
life as saga.

14

Memory is the manner in which I place myself in the American saga. Memory is one of the
ways which the saga shares its appositional power
with me. Memory coordinates the experience of
space and time. I can only exist in a hereness or
thereness which is measured by the degree in which
it is immediate to me. If it is very immediate, I
sense it as present. But the immediacy can be more
recollection that it is instanteneous; accordingly,
I sense it as past. If there is a degree of 'not-
yetness' to the immediacy, I sense it as future.
However, in terms of the actualities of experience,
the present, the past, and the future are all
sensibility to the immediacy in which existence is
encountered as space and time. Here-and-now, then-
and-there are always together. They are carried by
the character of life as saga.

Sometimes, when I scan the horizon of this
desert valley at night I forget that it is a desert.
I can look across the rolling rim of the mesa to the
lighted skyline beyond the Salt River Indian
Reservation. On all sides are the created filaments
of the culture zone, sparkling to send reassuring
signals telling me that all is well. Then comes the
daylight. On the edges of the pleasant flood of
sunshine I can see the dusty crags of the buttes and
the mountains. I still haven't gotten used to that
experience. For those uncommon elevations have a
way of seeming artificial to me, like papier maché
settings for some whimsical stage. It is as if I
could reach out to touch or replace them; but
it is part of their illusion to deceive me with
false impressions of their proximity. Perhaps
illusions isn't the word really. Daytime in the
desert, beyond the boundary of my simulated oasis,
reminds me that existence is precarious and proximate. Perhaps that's it: if I believe that
existence is illusion, it is because of my refusal
to accept the fact that life is an appositional
process, that I exist in interdependent realtion-
ship to all that is. To flee it as illusion is
just as false as to assume that the only reality is
the material order and what we make of it. The
desert confronts me with a threat to my identity.
I can so easily forget that the cities of humankind

are built along the perimeters of chaos. It takes
a failure of rainfall, a short circuit in the
currents of electrical power, to remind me that the
desert is hot, that it waits to reclaim the remains
of its sometime conquerors. I deal only in the
possibilities of this precarious moment. My
opportunities and resolutions are temporary and
proximate. They can never be final, ultimate, or
absolute. I cannot escape the actualities of
existence either by assuming that they are illusion,
or by trying to make them into an impregnable
fortress of achievement. Life is truly encountered
as saga, offering the source of equilibrium which
restores some measure of identity. For in its
moving narrative, it offers memory of a wholeness
that is much greater than my petty anxiety. The
wholeness of the saga carries the recollection of
streams, mountains, and forests as well as the
sands of chaos on which my house is built.

Hope, too, can never be illusion or
precise foreknowledge. Not that it does not pretend to be both these things much of the time.

> Hope never seems to leave those
>   who affirm,
> The shallow minds that stick to
>   must and mold--
> They dig with greedy hands for
>   gold
> And yet are happy if they find
>   a worm.

So said Dr. Faust to Wagner. We encounter hope in
ourselves and find it in others in much that is
naive, often evil, hoping "for gold." Hope is
frequently a looking forward to something better in
the future. Yet there is hardly a future which
does not present us with some desire to try hoping
again. There is disappointment in every future.
There is unanticipated evil or deprivation. And so
what can we do in such circumstance but "dig (again)
with greedy hands for gold?" If we pretend that
the unearthed worm is gold, we live in illusion--
our hope has been found wriggling in an unheroic
gesture of human pathos.

16

But there is another form of pretense that appears more valiant, more self-possessed. Since there is nothing but dread and fantasy in human hope, we must take full responsibility for the direction of the future. So says this second form of pretense. We can only avoid the shades of our undying narcosis by deciding what the dictates of our dream shall be. Design must follow desire; deed and discipline must come after decision. If gold is our hope, then it must be made. Of course, the result is that the availability of what we produce lessens its significance; or the ingredients become scarce and threaten a new crisis. Or, perhaps some intricate balance in the universe is toppled by the seeming insignificance of a simple act of manufactured hope.

Never mind all that! The problems of planned history, of future control are legion. But hope itself seems to insist on its right to exist. In Aldous Huxley's Brave New World, John the Savage, Bernard Marx, and Helmholtz Watson are the emergent aberrations of hope in a world that has sought to eliminate the need for hope. "Man's hopes are 'blind,' i.e., unintelligent and miscalculating, deceptive, and illusory," writes Karl Lowith, "And yet mortal man cannot live without this precarious gift of Zeus, as little as he can live without fire, the stolen gift of Prometheus." So we find a pattern for hope. We must discern a manner in which hope comes to us, is given to us. We must be able to hope without deluding ourselves into pretense about the future.

Somehow, the American saga suggests such a hope. Hope has always been a key factor in our consciousness and our experience. It brought ancient exiles to the shores of an unwitting hinterland. It drove the disenchanted from familiar discomforts into an unknown warring wilderness. Hope, deep within the mystery of America, linking soil and spirit, supported the children of the saga in the midst of storm and protest--through wars, depressions, panics; through corruption and oppression. Hope became revolution as well as consolation. No one can effectively deny that there

have been many moments in the saga when hope was
claimed by greedy hands, piling the waste of their
vulgar consumption on the helpless heads of the
powerless. The American saga has many distortions
of its theme. There are many perverse chapters.
But the unique combination of *universal* potential
and *particular* time and space that make up the
American experience is an organic process. The
saga offers the hope that brings freedom to the
oppressed through the vision of a fullness in the
American saga that is the right of all humankind.
Even protest is derived from the saga itself. The
American saga is a story of human mystery and meaning that includes all races, all of nature, and all
lesser accounts as important episodes. There is
hope because the American saga is not static, never
finally realized. The continuing story knows with
the Puritan fathers that "there is yet more light
to break forth." I do not live in illusion; I can
live in the *actualities* of the American saga. I do
not have to contrive the future, because the future
is present but never *wholly* present. It will be
part of the purpose of further chapters to clarify,
to demonstrate how this is so.

V.

I may be dissatisfied with certain elements in the saga. I may observe the injustice,
the heartless rapine thrust against the seeming
helplessness of the earth. But I cannot remove myself from the saga. If I do, I cease to exist in
any meaningful manner. For Americans, to exist is
to live in the American saga. For Americans, that
saga somehow touches the four directions of the
world and the complexions of time. But that is a
qualitative measure, not a quantitative one. It
does not mean that we are faced with the conquest
or evangelization of millions of the world's inhabitants. It means that the account of life's
mystery and meaning that makes up the American
experience has ultimately to do with all humanity.
In Paul Tillich's manner of discussing it, it means
that the particularities in the American saga will
break open to a more universal truth that is
present in the struggle and expectations of human-

kind.

The personal self comes into being to the
degree in which we have learned to respond to the
offered power of meaning that sets its relationships in apposition to us. That emergent self is
just as important as the appositional power itself.
Neither exists without the other; yet together they
demonstrate the fact that both selfhood and appositional power are always "more than" any given
definition, appropriation, or realization of them.
Life is participation and response, preserving both
the uniqueness of the individual and the more
universal context to which it relates. Even
Sigmund Freud, in his Future of an Illusion, says
"moreover, it is especially *apposite* to say that
civilization *gives the individual* these (religious)
ideas, for he finds them there already; they are
presented to him ready-made, and he would not be
able to discover them for himself" (italics mine).
Freud's is a half-truth, but an important first
step in understanding. Meaning certainly is
given, offered, found, presented. But not just by
something called civilization, not just in an
arbitrary fashion. And there is no power of meaning that is not so received rather than made; no
individuality that is not discovered in relational
terms.

When the Plains Indians perform the Sun
Dance, they are engaged in a quest for vision, as
well as in rites of renewed "communion with the
earth, sun, and the spirits, and especially with
the winds, so that the tribe might have health and
fertility and the buffalo might not fail."
Participation, in this case, signifies a kind of
response to all that gives meaning, of which one is
a part, and *by means* of which the self is enhanced.
For the quest for vision makes the participation
more than merely a subjugated functioning in some
mechanical process. And what is true for the
Plains Indian is true for all humanity. We are
essentially *participants.* We require some means of
effective and meaningful understanding of our
particpation in the saga of existence. From it we
derive both vision and communion. The American saga

19

includes the Indian, the Afro-American, the Latin American, as well as the spectrum of Oriental and European peoples who make up its consciousness. The larger sweep of the saga is as important to all of us as is the unique episode in which what we call ethnic, racial, or traditional patterns are discerned.

CHAPTER II

DISCERNING THE SOUL

I must confess that I never knew what soul really meant until the black man discovered it in the heart of the American saga. Saga--the intermingling of the stories of individuals and communities, struggling to relate the meaning of existence to the realities of space and time. And so the image of soul emerged. It had been there from the beginning and had assumed many forms. What never ceases to amaze me is the manner in which the discernments of our own day always find their paradigms earlier in the saga. For, while the 1960s evidenced the discovery of the "souls" of black folks, there is no denying the presence of that soul in the black preachers of the nineteenth century, and in the songs of freedom. As a matter of fact, soul knows no color; or rather, it knows *many* colors. What the black man and woman have shown us is what it means. They have demonstrated the *necessity* of discerning soul. They have danced their image of soul across the lifeless stage of our latter-day consciousness. And that dance, sometimes choreographed in defiance, is what helps us gain the discernment of soul we so desperately need today.

"Discernment," says John Dillenberger, "is an act of imagination. True imagination is not idleness nor slovenliness but carries its own discipline." Discernment is learning to be a critical observer *and* a compassionate participant. Presumably the ideal spectator at an athletic contest is one who has played the game. Yet what one observes from the seats of the stadium is a different form of truth from what is known in the heat of the contest. Both forms are turth; both valid; both necessary. Now, to a certain extent it may be assumed that discernment is a gift. It is present to the complexities of one's selfhood. It is "there" in one person in a manner seemingly not available to another. It has to do with the uniqueness and particularity of the individual. Perhaps

21

an individual age--an spoch--is possessed of a
climate of discernment just as is the individual
self. It is the quality that makes possible "discerning the signs of the times." But something
about discernment is also acquired through a dis-
ciplined act. Discernment is by the *experience* of
discernment. It is learning to see. Of course,
we all see in some measure. What it means is to
see-to have the senses touch and measure the
realities about us--that which is present to all
of us, even a blind person. But we are not fully
aware of what that "seeing" means until something
occurs that breaks through the routine of seeing,
forcing us out of our habitude in such a way that
we being to "see" what has been present to us
almost constantly. When that happens we begin to
practice the art of discernment. We are even
able to raise our sight from particular to more
universal truths.

        Strangely enough, that which breaks
through the routine of our seeing is usually an
encounter at the very horizon of our being. From
the depths of our existence we are pulled upward
and outward in joy or in suffering. The horizon
is changed; it has moved. The perimeters of
reality have shifted. "This is a story that
happened to me," said the Baal Shem Tov. "I was
riding in a coach drawn by three horses, each of a
different color, and not one of them was neighing.
I could not understand why. Until the day we
crossed a peasant on the road who shouted at me to
loosen the reins. And all at once, the horses
began to neigh." Elie Wiesel, who tells that
story of the Hasidic master, the Baal Shem Tov,
adds a word of interpretation: "For the soul to
vibrate and cry out, it must be freed; too many
restrictions will stifle it." The experience of
freedom is the extension of the horizon, the
loosening of the reins, that accompanies the vibration of the very limits of existence in joy or
sorrow. REcall for a moment how it is that someone
tells you his whole life has been changed by one
event. We encounter some beautiful embodiment of
physical attraction and personal charm, and in a
moment's vision the world changes--its horizons

shaped by love. Some sudden illness crashes into the consciousness and we see everything differently. Weeks, months, years have gone by; and all during that time the routine of our seeing has been undisturbed. Then in a brief moment, a repetition in time of the many that have gone before, the horizon is different. Why should it be that many years can be changed by one day? Perhaps we measure time incorrectly.

The dawn of discernment breaks forth when the horizons of the soul begin "to vibrate." Who can say which is first? Is it that the soul is the product of our discernment? Probably not. Is it then that the soul makes an urgent call for the art of discernment? Perhaps. But it is more likely true that the two are inseparable in cause and effect. For life is not cause and effect. It is saga, and the discernment of that fact is what reduces our alienation from the tyranny of events. We have discovered soul because we see for the first time that life is response.

What then is this soul that is discerned in the American saga? It is integreated selfhood, and integrated consciousness of human community. It is body and spirit together. "One of the unfortunate consequences of the intellectualization of man's spiritual life was that the word 'spirit' was lost and replaced by mind or intellect, and that the element of vitality which is present in 'spirit' was separated and interpreted as an independent biological force. Man was divided into a bloodless intellect and a meaningless vitality." So wrote Paul Tillich in one of his many attempts to reclaim the word 'spirit.' But what did he really *mean* by it? In his very next sentence he provided the key: "The middle ground between them, the spiritual *soul* in which *vitality* and intentionality are united, was dropped" (italics mine). Tillich was talking about what the Afro-American has known as "soul." The union of life process and human will, that is soul. The mind, the body, the will, the spirit--*together*, they make up what it means to discern the soul. To be able to dance with your whole self in moments of joy, that is

23

soul. To be able to feel your body and your mind,
your spirit, agonizing together in suffering, that
is soul. Reaching from the depth of being out to
the horizons of existence, in full vibration, that
is soul. For it really is acknowledgement of the
fact that there is no way out of the human condition. The horizon is there, but not as a line of
escape. Joy does not promise that life will now be
better. Suffering does not comfort us with the
assurance of its ending, or with the suggestion
that we are virtuous by our endurance. Joy and
suffering themselves remind us of what it is to be
human. They are themselves experiences of the
horizon of our being, confronting us with the fact
that we are not the makers of our own existence.
The black person, unfortunately, was *forced* to
discover that truth sooner than many others. He
discerned the soul that remained "on ice" for
others.

     The American saga is the story of the for-
mation of soul. That may seem a point of contention to some. There may be the suggestion that
certain non-literate peoples--perhaps African or
native American--can discern the human soul outside
the framework of the American saga. Possibly, but
not likely. "Primitive" affinity for the vitality
of nature is an important ingredient in the discernment of soul. But it is only *one-half* of the
process and tends to lead either to deterministic
participation in the routines of nature or else to
maddened possession by a plethora of natural
vitalities. Nothing ever breaks through the routine. There is no real horizon; rather, everything
is contained within the persistent pattern of
nature. As such there is no true intentionality,
no will. There is no history, no biography, no
story, no saga. Without a measure of freedom from
the conditions of nature, there is no intentionality. Thus, there is no achievement and in the
end no justice or injustice, no responsibility.

     But soul is the *union* of vitality and in-
tentionality. It makes a considerable difference
whether we simply sit in subjection to the vitalities of existence; or whether we discover that joy

24

and suffering are genuine reminders of who we are and that we are responsible beings. It is not that we shall escape the vitalities of existence by some technologically contrived selfhood. It is that we shall unite those vitalities with our freedom as humans. Unless we succumb to the deterministic pressures of technology, we currently seem to have the possibility for a new sensibility. Science and technology have been primarily intentionality. They have arisen out of the intentional process of the Western religious mind, which has been the bearer of Greek thought, and Hebraic action-metaphor. However, as we have seen, there is that aspect of the human journey which is represented by peoples like the African and native American. It, too, produces a determinism--a determinism of vitality. It is only when we encounter the tension between vitality and intentionality that soul is discerned and determinism of either sort is avoided. We begin to be truly human, and open to the power of meaning that offers itself to us. In a very real sense, of course, the discernment of soul has been present in the American saga from the beginning. The very nature of the saga as a continued realization of new levels of meaning suggests that there are diverse occasions in which body, mind, and spirit find integration.

The gentle Palatine Germans, who began their migration into the American saga almost before William Penn arrived in Pennsylvania, had known the suffering that the intentional mind inflicts on others. By way of their dispossession from their homeland they learned how the human pilgrimage is one of response to and participation in meanings that are given. We call them Pietists--those Germans--but that in no way means they were satisfied with the inner perfection of their hearts. For, they knew how to share the suffering of others. They had discerned the soul. Which is why, for example, they could oppose the enslavement of Africans.

In Chaim Potok's novel The Chosen, we are introduced to the tensions within Jewish life represented by the Hasidim and Orthodox Judaism.

25

Reb Saunders, the Hasidic Tzaddik, has raised his
son Danny in a tradition of silence. Through the
years he has not spoken to Danny except out of
necessity or in the course of studying Talmud together. Toward the end of the story Reb Saunders
reveals the reason for raising Danny in silence.
It was because he had discovered quite early that
Danny had a brilliant mind *with no soul*. Even a
great mind could be a shell that choked the possibility of soul that is available to each of us. As
a four-year-old, Danny had *enjoyed* stories that
spoke of Jewish suffering, but he had had no sensitivity to that suffering itself. He had *devoured*
the storeis with his mind. He was a mind in a body
with no soul. He had to be taught to look for the
horizons of his selfhood, to seek his own strength,
to suffer in order that he might find his woul.
The silence of his father had taught Danny the meaning of suffering; now he would be a man with a soul
no matter what he did with his life.

Whatever authentic selfhood is ever discerned must overcome the aggressive presumptions of
the mind and its feigned intentionality. For the
mind by itself can never lead to true intentionality. It exists in affectation, divorced from the
body, assuming that it can direct the self from the
lofty perch of its extrinsic superiority. But the
mind knows no honest intentionality by itself.
Right thinking or bad thinking--it matters not,
except as thinking. If there is no soul, it means
that true integrated selfhood is not a reality. It
is the soul that makes true intentionality possible
because it exists in creative tension with the
vitalities of our humanity.

It is worth a momentary digression to
suggest that many of today's problems in person-
ality adjustment and in national purpose are the
result of the failure to discern the soul. History
from the time of the Age of Reason to the era of
technocracy has produced minds without souls. The
process has been gradual, but it has been extremely
persistent.

26

Two Souls, alas are dwelling in my
        breast,
And one is striving to forsake its
        brother.
Unto the world in grossly loving
        zest,
With clinging tendrils, one adheres;
The other rises forcibly in quest
Of rarefied ancestral spheres.

Not really two *souls*, Doktor Faust, but two *minds*
struggling against the essential character of life.
If there were *soul* there would not be two. There
would be integrated selfhood. That is why the so-
called simple man, he who is of "the folk", frequently is much more of a "soul" than the most
learned intellectual. And we must find a way of
ridding ourselves of the notion that the mind as
mind is a superior reality. It is in fact a lesser
reality than the "soul", for he who has "soul" is
wise. And wisdom is much to be desired.

        Before we discover wisdom of the soul, we
assume that life's meaning is entirely of our own
making, or that existence can be escaped by a
superior mind or a transformed spirit. Or perhaps,
we try to protect ourselves from full humanity by
residing in the shelters of nature's drives and
cycles. Only the reality of the saga can prevent
that, because saga is itself much larger than
natural vitality and contriving mind. Saga itself
is the union of life-process and human will. The
American saga is irreducible. It is not just
nature's way; nor is it human construction--even
though both of those elements are present within
the saga. In the flow of the dark beginnings and
the expanding horizons we discern the soul of our
peoplehood and our personal souls. If we never
discover the saga, our struggle for integration as
individuals and responsible direction as a people
will never be achieved. Rather we shall continue
to be wandering, fragmented creatures, at war with
ourselves and iwth others. The therapies of
diverse psycho-theories and political machination
will be at best illusive and at worst aggressively
presumptuous.

Soul is discerned when we encounter the reality of the coincidence of opposites. Certain philosophers and historians like Mircea Eliade, Kees Bolle, and Louis Dupre have been documenting the necessity of the "coincidence of opposites" for and understanding of the history of religions or of the philosopher's task. What is frequently missed, however, is the simple fact that *any real account of life* is precisely that--a story of the coincidence of opposites. Life is lived as a coincidence of opposites; and any story that is told, fictional or otherwise, is a portrayal of that reality. To the extent that we are aware of that coincidence, we have discerned soul and are integrated beings. The problem is that most of us (intellectuals especially) fail to discover the saga and our participation in it. We want to erect a structure that takes no account of opposites--except as that opposite which aggravates us from the wrong side of our right. It is highly unlikely that soul is ever discerned among those who build systems and arguments that have no room for opposites. They deny the fundamental character of life--that it is saga. Much of modern civilization is such a denial.

I look out on Phoenix, this vast and sprawling metropolis in the midst of the Arizona desert. I see it growing, growing, until the edges of its triumph blot out the reminders of chaos. Life goes on as if we lived on the shores of Lake Michigan. Then comes the summer and the temperature rises to 118 or 120 degrees. The irrigation waters snake their way from canals and tunnels, gushing up through the sleuces to wash the grass and soak the roots of trees. All is well, yet how dependent, how precarious! And this desert metropolis is but an extreme demonstration of the whole of our technological society. We have tried to erect a fictitious world, based on the isolation of certain ideas, demands, and possibilities. But the opposites to all of those assumptions have been ignored. What we have done with the desert stands as a parable. For our world is an edifice created out of the attempt at the elimination of opposites. Why else do we find ourselves facing one technological crisis after another? Technology is the

architect of crisis. It must decide on a given pro-
cedure, a given manipulation of substance and method,
in order to achieve a certain desired result. But
what has been ignored in the process still exists;
and what has been fabricated by a process that
eliminated other factors will be hounded by those
neglected elements. There is no way to "solve a
problem" or "create a new product" without distort-
ing the basic balance in which opposites co-exist;
and the point is that the opposites are not eradi-
cated by being disregarded.

        I recall Edwin Corle's novel Fig Tree
John, the story of an old Apache facing the winds of
change. He and some fellow Indians from other
tribes are swapping tales around a campfire. They
talk about the Colorado River, and they laugh at the
white man who has disturbed the river by damming it
up, changing its course into the desert. The River
God will stand such nonsense only for so long, they
say, then the laugh will be on the stupid white man.
I think there are other than the River Gods who will
be aggravated. The Sky God, too, usually so far
removed from everything--he feels his breathing
agitated by warm airs that used to be moderate, by
moist acrid winds that once were soothing and dry.
Our science and technology must find a new foundation on which to build their schemes. Every theory
and application must defer to the coincidence of
opposites rather than attempt to eliminate one or
the other.

        The most terrible and yet most important
war in the span of the American experience is a
demonstration of that truth. There was a growing
number of states during the 1850s, and there was
also a growing consciousness of national *unity* and
purpose. Could each state be given absolute control
over its destiny and its people? Or should the
federal union prescribe the fate of all states? To
have replied with an unequivocal yes to the first
question would have eliminated the effective reality
of its opposite. And to have provided the federal
government with absolute determination would have
eliminated the states. But the American saga is an
account of the coincidence of opposites. We bear

witness to a balanced consciousness that reflects
practical circumstance: we are individual states
with identity and correspondent power; *and* we are a
united people with a greater identity than statehood
provides. There is particularized identity and
power, but it does not exist without the apparent
opposite of a more universal identity and power.

Something must hold together in meaningful
fashion what are in fact the realities of existence.
Only the saga can do that. If each of us had his
own way, we would try to purge the saga. By our
superior intellect, our moral excellence, or our
strength and technique we would prefer to dispose of
what is to us apparently ignorant, evil, weak or un-
skilled. And so we would ignore the possibility of
our own partial insights and abilities. We would
condition the present and the future and obliterate
human freedom. There would be no renewal of
existence, no surprises, no joy and perhaps no
sorrow. Only if there is the saga that contains all
possibilities in creative passage can there be a
future. For the saga is the guarantee against our
absolute conditioning. It offers us soul rather
than contrived subsistence. Life and death, day and
night, good and evil, creativity and destructivity--
the opposites are many. Soul represents the integrated and creative response to those opposites.

Not long ago I awoke to a rare experience
in our part of Arizona: it was a *cloudy day*. Some
genuises tell us that cloudy days are the only kind
of weather conducive to creative labors. Fog and
rain, clouds and heavy atmosphere--these are the
agitations that complement our natural human
anxieties and evoke expressions of beauty and inven-
tion. The Arizona desert conjures visions of
tranquility and lazy siestas under palms and palo
verde trees. I can assure you that my mood is much
different from what it was during my decades of
Pennsylvanian incubation. I like sunshine; and I
like to sit outdoors, writing at a table where these
words are being penned. But there is sadness here,
too; there is melancholy in the sunshine, even with
the bravado of the mocking bird and the nightingale,
the twittering bounce of the cactus wren, and the

ever-present world-rhythm of the turtledove. That
cloudy morning my daughter came running to me,
tears streaming down her cheeks. On the rug on the
patio floor, just outside the arcadia door, was a
bird. Fragments of her feathers were splattered
like glue against the glass. The poor little
creature was motionless, seemingly conscious--her
eyes open. Had she been stunned? Were her wings
broken? Were there internal injuries too great
to observe? We placed her at what we felt was a
safe spot, away from neighborhood cats. And there
was a little girl's prescription left by her side--
milk and water, saucered for easy treatment. But
the next morning the little spirit had returned to
a greater spirit. The bird was dead and there was
great mourning by two little girls.

      I have thought about that incident many
times. I know that somehow that bird probably saw
reflections in the large expanse of glass--reflec-
tions that led her to assume that there was no
obstacle in the path of her flight. But I chose to
think more of it than that. I believe the atmosphere
of that particular day was so different from the
ordinary that the little sparrow was not prepared for
what the *opposite* kind of atmosphere does to perception. As a creature of the sunny desert, she had no
means of adjustment that permitted the coincidence--
the side-by-sideness--of opposites. The singularity
of her responses led to destruction. True human
perception is a product of soul--that integrated
acceptance of opposites that represents wholeness--
salvation if you will. Only if I live with some
sense of participation in a saga will that integration take place.

            Nobody picks a red rose when the winter
               wind howls and the white snow blows
               among the fences and storm doors
            Nobody watches the dreamy sculptures of
               snow when the summer roses blow red
               and soft in the garden yards and
               corners.
            I have loved red roses and O I have
               loved white snow--dreamy drifts

31

winter and summer--roses and snow.

Carl Sandburg knew that deepening of the self, that
throbbing of the quick and the dead that pulses
along the American trail. It is sad and happy,
bold and hesitant--always the opposites! That is
what America *meant* to him. After all, the
cyclical intensity of the life force, the lust and
the weariness of it all--that must be balanced by
the freedom to move on, the intention to build and
create. The grandeur and misery of humanity is at
its profound heights in the American saga. And
there is no true humanity without grandeur and
misery.

> "People, Yes," said Sandburg,
>   The people will live on.
>   The learning and blundering people
>   will live on. (those opposites)
>   They will be tucked and sold and
>   again sold
>   And go back to the nourishing earth
>   for rootholds,
>   The people so peculiar in renewal
>   and comeback,
>   You can't laugh off their capacity
>   to take it.
>   The mammoth rests between his
>   cyclonic drama.

"The People, yes"--they know without
"methodologies" or dissertations about the *coinci-
dentia oppositorum* of the scholars. When I remember the simple Pennsylvania German farmers of my
youth, I can sense the meaning of those barn designs
and the decorative artistry of blanket chests and
iron ware. Figures of men, women, and children
intermingled with intellectual designs of turtle-
doves and lilies, of geometric intensity. I say
"intellectual design" because the art of these folks,
as John Joseph Stoudt has pointed out, is not representational; it is a product of articulate thought
and feeling. It is an artistry of life, bringing
images from the dark beginnings of the dimly
remembered past into the flow of the American saga.
Those folk were not a wealthy people, an aristocratic

gentry. They were a dispossessed, but an integrated,
people--a single organism, sharing, believing,
hoping, and celebrating as one. And their oneness
was in each individual as well as in their communal
selfhood. Only the American saga was old enough,
free enough and directional enough to permit that
integration.
                              IV.
        What we call imagination, faith, and
reason are all integrated realities in the American
saga. The appositional posture knows no distinctions like faith, reason, and imagination. These
latter are the products of the fragmentation of selfhood. They result from those madcap convulsions
since the Renaissance when human nature found itself
dissected into choice morsels of reason, nature, and
ideal. But the process has made for a series of
rather costly purchases in the marketplace of
modernity. For what Martin Lings says of Renaissance
art serves as an effective observation on the world
of culture since that time: "If Renaissance art
lacks an opening on to the universal and is altogether imprisoned in its own epoch, this is because its
outlook is humanistic; and humanism, which is a
revolt of the reason against the intellect, considers
man and other earthly objects entirely for their own
sakes as if nothing lay behind them." This form of
humanism has been in revolt against the intellect
ever since the Renaissance. And so we have the
struggles between imagination, faith, and reason.
Little do we recognize that such humanism is not
human, but mechanical and fractional.

        What is imagination but the manner in
which we create and respond to images that help us
to discern the meaning of things. What is it but
the sensibility that elicits wonder, inspiration,
and the motivation to express our existence in
gratefulness or in purposeful response? And then
what of faith? It is the "encompassing perspective,"
says John Dillenberger, "from which all that is said
is seen..." Faith is the fundamental knowledge of
trust and loyalty that serves as the milieu in which
imagination and reason are inseparable because life
is appositional--a story, a pattern of response to
the power of relational meanings that sacrifice

                              33

themselves in offering for us, and of which we require sacrifice in order to be individual humans.
That is our condition. But it means that there
can be no ultimate fragmentation of our faculties.
We play games with the separations of faith,
reason, and imagination. The consequence is disintegration, inability to discern the soul.

Why is it that the world of religious
scholarship has recently been discussing "story"
as a category of thought--as if something new had
been discovered? From the very beginnings of
humankind, many thinkers have been aware of the
superiority of story to any other form of truth-
accounting. It includes faith, imagination, and
reason--the combination that gives us soul. When a
students asks me a question, I begin that tedious
conceptual struggle that frequently works its way
to the blackboard in a series of words and diagrams.
Usually after I have finished one of my conceptual
structures, I remember too late the superiority of
story. The stories of the Buddha, of the Sufis,
the parables of Jesus, the tales of the Hasidim,
even the dialogues of Plato--how superior they are
to analects and codes, to critiques of pure and
practical reason, to phenomenologies and discourses.
Although it may be a bit too strident, I think of
Elie Wiesel's account of Israel of Rizhin's dislike
for Maimonides, the philosopher: "I'll tell you why.
Theoretically I should like him, for he refutes
Aristotle's theories, so dangerous for the faith.
But imagine Jews like you and me reading Aristotle's
theories in Maimonides' work and falling asleep
before he refutes them?" If only I could remember
the superior truth of story!

When a human being experiences *teshuvah* or
conversion, it is never because he has been
convinced by someone's argument, by the brilliance
of someone's reasoning. It is rather because his
faith, imagination, and reason have been set in
tune by a story that has a place for him. The
artist discerns soul; he discovers the faith that
sets images in motion in such a way that his reasoning mind can only express itself as part of his
total self. The revivalist of the 19th century, in

34

his crude simplicity, knew that human beings were
not naked ambulatory cerebra lying in ambush or
plotting a brazen streak across forbidden perimeters. The revivalist knew that reason must be
provided with a context of faith and imagination
that create the soul--the willing, directed,
integrated soul.

In an unusual way, what we most often
mean by story can be too biographical, too sub-
jective. That is precisely what frequently
happened in the revivalistic patterns of the 19th
century. It was too often a case of "Jesus and I,
hand in hand, going down life's road in eternal,
blissful harmony." Story must be derived from,
and be part of, saga. In the saga there are
objective, historical, and community dimensions
of reality which protect the story from smugness,
sentimentality, and narrow subjectivism. Saga
even goes beyond nationalism. Nationalism
is subjectivism blown to super-egotistical proportions. It is the particular pretending to be
universal. There is no soul in nationalism,
only vulgar intentionality and will-to-power.
The American saga is realted to the geography and
times that make up our history, but it is in no
way confined to such narrow proportions. Instead
it is a demonstration of the fact that any
encounter of meaning, any integration of soul,
occurs in relation to a specific and continuing
set of symbols that are held together in meaningful narrative.

"In our concern to go beyond nationalism,"
wrote Bernard Meland, "we need to guard against the
temptation to veer toward a sentimental universalism
that indiscriminately embraces foreign cultures and
depreciates the local culture." We cannot escape
our skins; without them there is no soul. Therefore, there is no escaping the American saga. In
fact, in its richness, in its movement toward the
future it "embraces foreign cultures." The interpreters of Manifest Destiny had the proper symbol;
they simply held a myopic interpretation. For the
embrace that has already begun to take place is not
one of political imperialism at all, although some

misguided politicians and industrialists may see it
so. No, the embrace occurs as the symbols in our
saga breaks through their particularity and meet the
broken particularities of other cultures. The
embrace occurs as others begin to discover that
their self-affirmation and liberation are part of
the account that was released when the American
saga began to be told.

V.

Soul is the creative interaction of judgment and reconciliation in our experience. "Something there is that doesn't love a wall," wrote
Robert Frost, "That sends the frozen-grown-swell
under it, and spills the upper boulders in the sun;
and makes gaps even two can pass abreast." But
walls there are, and probably always shall be; and
"something there is" that will reveal the common
ground beneath. Walls are a form of judgment, of
discrimination—inevitable in the human settlement.
And when I see a wall, I have to wonder, with Frost:
Why is it there? What is being walled in and out?
Imaginary walls there are, but no, not imaginary—
invisible, but walls as rigid as the red granite
blocks that set my yard off from my neighbor's.
Invisible walls that say, "Chicanos belong here;
blacks belong there." Women can pass between the
gates in the walls behind which blacks, and reds,
and Mexican-Americans live their time. But women
run into subtle walls that weave like the maze
created by some mad behaviorist, the fencing woven
through the crannies of crackling compounds left
by other builders.

I recall years ago reading Walter Prescott
Webb's The Great Plains. What a marvellous book it
is! I can remember the terror I felt at his
description of that vast sea of imageless prairie
flatland. No landmarks—nothing so far as the eye
could see. Imagine, if you can, the aimlessness,
the loneliness. There were those who moved in endless circles that became wheels of insanity, of
vertigo, physical illness. A wall is a mark for
distinguishing reality. It helps us find directions.
It helps us identify; it is a way of thinking. With-

36

out walls we might not be human at all. Mircea Eliade has shown us that utter homogeneity of experience can have no conception of space or time. It is the heterogeneous breakthrough of the sacred that provides the sightings for space and the recollections for time. The experience of irruption is judgment. It enables us to build a wall; it provides us with a principle for judging, discriminating. And sometimes that judgment is harsh. It is harsh if we have permitted the homogeneity of things to blind us to injustice. It is severe if we have ignored the fact that the walls of judgment we have created are not absolutes, they are never to be permitted to obscure the fact that "something there is that doesn't love a wall." Every judgment makes sense only in relation to the possibility for an advance in the universal relationship of humans with each other and with nature. Beneath every wall of judgment and discrimination there is the common ground that made the discriminating necessary in the first place, and that will demand our constant attention to it. For the common ground lives in creative tension with the walls on its surface. Therefore every wall of judgment exists in relation to the common ground of necessary reconciliation.

What I am suggesting is that there must be a constant passage of judgment and reconciliation in human experience. There is soul when the judgment on my present achievement and understanding is followed by some reconciliation to a continuing possibility. There is soul when the judgment on the achievement and understanding of others permits a form of reconciliation that allows our commonality to express itself. The discernment of that soul tells us that all is well--that a future is already upon us. The American saga carries the power of meaning of that fundamental truth. Abraham Lincoln knew that no *one side* ever wins. In no way can my own judgment of my rights and expectations be considered the whole truth. The truth is in the saga.

CHAPTER III

INVITATION TO THE PROMISED LAND

I have tried to imagine what was in the mind of the first Asian who looked across the Bering Strait. Was he running *from* something or *to* something? How much of a commission had he been given for his assignment? Was it the gods who had told him that the direction of his journey was through the frozen twilight into the hospitality of a promised land? Did he know that he was making a pilgrimage that might take many ages, that his passage was away from all he had known into a world that existed only in promise? And was he aware of the fact that the *end* of it all was like returning home to the land of the gods? How different can his vision have been from that of the first European who grazed the shores and inlets of the Atlantic coastline? How different from what was in the minds of those aboard the Arbella, prepared to erect their city upon a hill that must have appeared somewhat foreboding? The difference is in the span of time and in the language that tries to express such thoughts. But the images must have been a pattern. In the saga of the American soul there is the image of the invitation to the promised land, without which we are certainly less than human.

In the first place, the image is one of liberation. If the American consciousness is stalemated at the moment, it is partially because we have been at ease in our captivity. A subtle slavery it is, of course, this "brave new world" of ours. Our wants and our needs are profoundly conditioned at every hand by the commercial positivism of our day. Carl E. Braaten has suggested that a rule frequently applied in his family is: if you've seen it on television, you don't need it. However, it isn't that easy to avoid power, and the dominant form of power of our time is commercial positivism, the meaning of which is simple: the only adequate reality is that which consumes and responds to the controls of consumption. The application of this positivism is dominant in government and in education, as well as in the usual marketplace. The shopping mall is the model of such a culture; for it suggests that it is the center of life, where taste is defined and needs are met. We take our leisure-world stroll along the air-conditioned avenues of the malls, past contrived gardens and carefully designed cages with tropical birds and entertaining monkeys. At the hub of the microcosm of this universe is a refreshing fountain--a fictitious well-spring where people sit to rest their feet and contemplate their checkbook balance or the terrors of next month's credit-card billing. But there before them is an art exhibit, where some of the best painters, ceramicists, and jewelry-craftsmen display their work. All of this, mind you, in a huge temple complex which defines your role as a supplicant to the value system. Even the occasional artist, who thinks he is free in his expression and his life-style, sits among the vendors and hopes that the money-changers will render his prophecy worth of its hire.

"We are living through the experience of a closed world," say Jacques Ellul. "Never have there been so many openings, scientific break-throughs by the most stupefying, lightning-like extentions of technology, the secularization of thought and of civilization, the opening of doors to 'the cosmos'; yet never has man felt so closed in, so confined, so impotent." It should come as not real surprise to us that that is *as much* a description of the general human condition as it is a characterization of this moment of our history. Notice, I have said "as much" because I wish in no way to detract from the seriousness, indeed, the uniqueness of Ellul's masterful analysis of our present captivity. However, I recall Loren Eiseley's discussion of "the cosmic prison" in The Invisible Pyramid, where he describes the naivete of those who saw the first moon landing as an indication of the human ability to chart our own course, play our own freedom, "go anywhere we choose." But Eiseley prudently describes the reality of our situation: "To escape the cosmic prison man is poorly equipped." Needless to say, our captivity of the moment is real even if our awareness of it is at low ebb. We have been for

40

some time in process of being victimized by the
mentality of the shopping mall. Government in our
time seems to function according to a principle in
which efficient management is the supreme value.
Executive government has been understood to mean
the control of the culture by impersonal disregard
of any other values. We have been envisioned as
consuming beings who require absolute manipulation
at all levels. The horror and pathos of the whole
episode is that the perpetrators of this obscenity
have been unaware of their own captivity, therefore,
likewise insensible to their actions.

        The resultant unethical behaviour in
government is not the result of any notion of
America's unique role and opportunity. The would-
be prophets, frustrated by their own helplessness,
gesture madly and thump their breasts crying "mea
culpa" for all of America. But there is no power
in their gesture and there is little wisdom in
their actions. It is not because there are images
that arise from the American saga that we are in
trouble. It is rather because human beings who
are not truly sensible to the appositional character of life proceed to assault life, to manipulate
and control it, rather than respond gracefully to
it. Or, to put it another way: when we do not
realize that we are the participants in a saga that
offers meaning to us, is greater than we *are* or
understand, greater than we can envision or bring
into realization at any one moment, *then* we take
the images and try to reduce them to instruments of
assault and control. But we know in the depth of
our being, just as we see at the horizons of our
existence, that images cannot be so reduced. Since
they are really prior to thought and action we
simply cripple ourselves in the mistaken manipulation of their power. Of course, we are constantly
tempted to do this with our lives. Surely our
minds, our physical prowess, our cunning, our
craftsmenship can reduce the saga and its images to
our own proportions: so we constantly think. In
feigned humility, Mephistopheles says to us as to
Faust:

41

"I'm not one of the great,
But if you want to make your way
Through the world with me united,
I should surely be delighted
To be yours, as of now,
Your companion, if you allow;
And if you like the way I behave,
I shall be your servant, or your slave."

The image of the Promised Land suggests
something different. It tells us that the future
depends upon our willingness to risk some of the
comfort of the present, which has deceived us into
captivity. To the Hebrew expatriates from old Egypt
there was a certain amount of anxiety connected with
leaving at least some shade, some water and a crust
of bread for an uncertain death in a desert wilderness in search of a Promised Land. With liberation
comes risk and that is not an easy quality to find
today. There must come into existence a community
of those who know the American saga well enough to
risk present captive security for a Promised Land.
Those who will take the risk are those who are
willing to live by promise. It is a going forth,
like a pilgrim, not knowing when death shall come,
but enjoying the freedom of the promise. For the
pilgrim there are sightings of land, occasional
shrines and chapels, in which the promise is renewed
by a foretaste of its plentitude. He is never
finally deceived by any mirage, nor is he prey to
the temptation to settle in any shrine along the way
as its resident high priest. He is a human on the
move, in liberation, living by promise. The
Promised Land is not for the rich, but for the poor
and dispossessed. And we must reclaim that image
for America. There will be a day when the kings,
and the corporate manipulators--the control figures
in the prison of our commercial positivism--shall be
brought low. Meanwhile we must set sail aboard the
ships that will take us out of the citadels of
slavery. Whether it be with Ponce de Leon, with
John Winthrop and the Massachusetts Bay Company, or
with the black slave preacher--we shall all travel
in freedom. We shall all have much to learn, we
shall not be perfect; but we shall be humans of
wisdom. More than a matter of skill and great

knowledge, the image of the Promised Land is the wisdom of those who know that what is yet to come frees us from any enslavement to the one-dimensional reality of the present.

Perhaps we live with a strange commonplace --almost a caricature of those who know the power of the image of the Promised Land. We may think they are fools who wait for the stereotypical illusion of celestial pastry. But do you really suppose the black slave preacher thought only to console his misery when he saw his people like the children of Israel--soon to be led into a land flowing with milk and honey? He was seldom such a fool as that! He was a wise man. He knew, in ways that many of us forget, that there is freedom for the present and promise of a wholly new dispensation for those who are sensible to the movement of the saga of existence.

Or what of the children of Jamestown or Plymouth? Shall we suppose they left the confines of the one-dimensional reality of Europe only to disembark completely disenchanted on the strands of Hell's perimeters? Surely there was disappointment; there was the same kind of suffering that has always given rise to the cry of dereliction: "My God, my God; why hast thou forsaken me? Why did I ever go on such a foolish journey?" I cannot imagine anyone who truly knows the image of the Promised Land ever saying: "Well, we've been at it for a year now! There certainly is no milk and honey in this tone quarry! What kind of wild goose chase has this been?"

> Should God give you worlds, and
> laws, and treasures, and world
> upon worlds, and Himself also
> in the Divinest manner, if you
> will be lazy and not meditate you
> lose all. The soul is made for
> action, and cannot rest till it
> be employed. Idleness is its rust.
> Unless it will up and think and
> taste and see, all is in vain.

43

> Worlds of beauty and treasure
> and felicity may be round about
> it, and itself desolate. If
> therefore you would be happy,
> your life must be as full of
> operation as God of treasure.

So wrote Thomas Traherne, reminding us that there is no soul except in terms of active thrust into worlds that are beyond the clouds on our horizon. We can speak meaningfully of the saga of the American soul because there is present in it an image of the Promised Land that enables us to operate consciously quite beyond the present horizon.

II.

The Promised Land is a concrete and realistic image. It refers to a promised *land*. What is promised is not just promise itself. What is involved is not simply vision or the experience of another reality than the world of technocracy or commercial positivism. However we may be drawn in liberation from our present captivity, it can never result in a separation from nature. The power of the promise may cause us to see nature differently, but it will also suggest that the consummation of any future will include nature itself. The earth, the unfathomable depths of space, the sisterhood of water and life--they are the milieu in which our promise is fulfilled. In one sense that is an observation that seems available to us from nature itself. "The giant confined in the body's prison," says Loren Eiseley, "roams at will among the stars. More rarely and more beautifully, perhaps, the profound mind in the close prison projects infinite love in a finite room. This is a crossing beside which light-years are meaningless. It is the solitary key to the prison that is man."

From beyond the horizon, where only promise beckons us--do we not see More Than the prison? And when Eiseley writes of that projection of "infinite love," is it really only the projection of a profound mind? Or is it perhaps a transformed mind? For a finite mind cannot project anything

44

infinite. It can only respond to an infinite; which
means that it must be transformed from its custom of
seeing all reality as projection *within* the cosmic
prison. Transformation occurs when human intentionality has been liberated from the ordinary mind with
all of its profundity and stupidity. Transformation
occurs when we are grasped by the power of an image
that transcends the narrow interrelationships of
most thought. The projection of "infinite love in
a finite room" is an event quite beyond the ordinary
capacities of the finite room, the cosmic prison of
nature. It is a projection of the finite room
itself into a future that is born out of response to
a promise, a promise that sees a transformed nature,
but a *real* land nevertheless.

In Stephen Vincent Benet's "Invocation" to
John Brown's Body, there is depicted the great
diversity of experience with the land that could
never be reduced to the prescriptions of any
ideological or ethnic attempt to contain it.

> American muse, whose strong and diverse
>   heart
> So many men have tried to understand
> But only made it smaller with their art,
> *Because you are as various as your land*
>   (italics mine)
> As mountainous--deep, as flowered with
>   blue rivers,
> Thirsty with deserts, buried under
>   snows,
> As native as the shape of Navajo
>   quivers,
> And native, too, as the sea-voyaged
>   rose.

We may have forgotten that the promise must include
the land, but there is no final forgetting that can
erase the ultimate meaning of the image. For, it is
as

> a friend, an enemy, a sacred hag
> With two tied oceans in her medicine-
>   bag.

I wonder how we can ever suppose that the Promised
Land is only a lingering fantasy of our immaturity.
It is as essential, as operative, an image today as
it ever could have been for those who crowded ships
from other shores, or dreamed of planned escape
from under iron heels.

> The maimed presumption, the unskilful
>   skill,
> The patchwork colors, fading from the
>   first,
> And all the fire that fretted at the
>   will
> With such a barren ecstasy of thirst.
> Receive them all--and should you
>   choose to touch them
> With one slant ray of quick, American
>   light,
> Even the dust will have no power to
>   smutch them,
> Even the worst will glitter in the
>   night.

We are less than human if the Promised
Land casts no image into the crucible of our
thought and imagination. If we seem to have filled
the American land with savage encampments of greedy
mercenaries; if from the majesty of our mountains
the purple now lingers in somnolent haze; if the
waters gurgle in the throes of retching agony; if
the frontier is no more; then it is time for us to
confront the real meaning of the Promised Land.

The promise demands vision, responsibility,
and hope. These are qualities that carry the image
even beyond the scope of American shores. The world
shares at every point in East and West the same
capacity for corruption and distortion; it has the
same needs, the same desires that make the earth a
wasteland. "A philosophic and religious Orient,"
wrote Reinhold Niebuhr, "permits millions to perish
in poverty. An energetic and busy West spills
rivers of blood in the mad scramble for the world's
riches. The Western man must bring his energy under
moral control. The Eastern man must learn the moral
value of energy." But Western humanity has no

46

priority over the potentialities of greed; and the nations of the world begin to display common characteristics of human nature once they discover effective methods for exploiting lands and people. But knowledge is always power, whatever else it may be. And power is the awareness of the strength of one's consciousness or position. It is power that is most demonstrative of the alienation that lies beneath the surface of the human condition. We must be fully cognizant of the fact that technology has begun the long process that will make us more aware of the universality of the alienation in human nature. The nobility of Hindu thought and the tenacity of Islamic morality will not prevent the use of power for gain or preservation. Technology makes visible the universal human condition. We have frequently called this process secularization. But somehow that term has a mostly negative connotation--getting rid of the vestiges of the sacred. Its positive side, of course, is that it presumably frees us for full human responsibility. Actually, all that the process accomplishes is a demonstration of the universality of our tendency to use whatever power is available to us for our own ends. We cannot expect India to be any more pacifist than we are, just as we cannot expect an African or Latin American nation to be satisfied with the richness of some euphoric simple life which our counter-cultural melancholy longs for in the midst of the frustrations of complexity.

If we have looked for the Promised Land with too sharply defined a charting of its specifications, we are in trouble. Such charting leads to illusion about who we are and what we have a right to expect of our human pilgrimage. It leads to assault rather than graceful response; in effect it represents a rejection of the appositional character of reality. The image of the Promised Land associates promise with the relationship of humanity and nature. It is symbolic of the fact that we cannot "construct" such a land, nor can we envision it precisely. It is illusory to do so. So at this moment in the continuity of the American saga we are being reminded that we are not free to live with any such illusion. There is no future, no hope, unless

47

that illusion vanishes. The illusion imprisons us, permits us to accept the conditioning security of a present commercial positivism. It makes us want to assume that the synthetic milk and honey of the shopping mall are the land toward which we have been led. The result of such an assumption is that we contribute no understanding of the real meaning of the saga to the rest of the world. We offer no realistic comprehension of what it means to be human and we provide no image beyond the illusory character of our conditioned security. Accordingly, the rest of the world moves in the direction of our present illusion, with the same factitious expectations.

We should have learned long since that "Human nature is...a realm of infinite possibilities of good and evil because of the character of human freedom. The love which is the law of its nature is a boundless self-giving. The sin which corrupts its life is a boundless assertion of the self." Or, as Niebuhr said elsewhere: "Freed from...illusions we have every possibility of perfecting the justice of social institutions." The image of the Promised Land suggests to us that we must begin to view our future as a gift, the meaning of which comes to us as a different dimension of reality from what we are accustomed. We are freed from illusions about the present or the contrivance of an absolute future only by an image like the Promised Land, which repeats to us the "not yet, but look, see the horizon is already in the midst of your vision." We are freed to do presently what is required of us --to live as children of the Promised Land. If we know that the truth of reality is a gift, that the Promised Land is not on our terms, then we begin to live in communion with nature and technological possibility by means of a new style.

The Sioux asked forgiveness of the buffalo as he fell from the deadly thrust of the arrow. The Hopi seeks the forgiveness of the snake, slain by the wheels of his pickup truck. Whether derived of the necessity for food or the accidents of existence, the American Indian is aware that the future is always dependent upon the depths of his relationships

48

with the brothers and sisters of nature. Of course,
to some extent that is the propensity of the so-
called nature mystic; and Christians know that
St. Francis is the paradigm for a similar mode of
living. But it is useless to suppose that we can
revert to the life-style of the Hopis, or practice
the presence of St. Francis in what Herbert Richardson calls a sociotechnic culture. We may be able to
develop personal patterns of behavior that reflect
our sensibility to the fact that the Promise of the
future includes the animal and plant kingdom. But
when we realize that all peoples--*including* the
American Indians--are measuring their future and
their independence by the standards of commercial
positivism (they want *their own* shopping mall
existence), we must be wary of any life-style that
may be purely sentimental.   .

The Promised Land will include nature,
but it cannot ignore the evils or the potential of
technology. Needless to say, however, the image of
the Promised Land we have been describing robs
technology of its totalitarian claims just as it
suggests the futility of any reactionary primitivism.
It would be indeed strange to discover that many
white Americans had begun to play Indian, Hindu, or
African, at the very moment when the Indian, the
Hindu, and the African grasp the instrumentalities
of technological power.

Jonathan Edwards knew that the salvation
he preached during the great awakenings of the
eighteenth century was part of a redemption that
included the realms of nature. He believed that
America itself was the setting in which the image
of the Kingdom of God would have its realization.
His salvation was not some escape into a heaven
beyond the miseries of existence. Nor, on the
other hand, was it some final product of human
ingenuity. The realization is here *in this land*,
but it is a realization that is never completed
according to our schedule. Therefore, it is
always open ended. The image of the Promised
Land reminds us that there is an element of transcendence about the future, yet it is a future that
has to do with the nature and destiny of life as

49

we know it. *This is the land of promise* to which we must open our minds and our hearts. In response to such an image our technology becomes a celebration of the saga in which we live. It becomes the building of ceremonial cities and canals. It becomes the ritual of a liturgy that draws humanity and nature together into a celebration of the future.

The American saga bears the image of the Promised Land for all peoples. If the promise was once claimed by the narrow instincts of Anglo-Saxons, it demonstrated its greater power and meaning by serving as the symbol of liberation for the black man, as the foundation of claims for equality by eastern Europeans. Hector St. John de Crevecoeur, in his description of the American--even before the time of the War for Independence--stated the case extravagantly: "No sooner does an European arrive, no matter of what condition, than his eyes are opened upon the fair prospect: he hears his language spoke: he retraces many of his own country manners; he perpetually hears the names of families and towns with which he is acquainted; he sees happiness and prosperity in all places disseminated; he meets with hospitality, kindness, and plenty everywhere; he beholds hardly any poor; he seldom hears of punishments and executions; and he wonders at the elegance of our towns, those miracles of industry and freedom." Needless to say, the portrait is a bit over-sketched, even for its own time. But there is evidence arising to show that even the Roman Catholic missions of the South-west, prior to the time of the military usurpation, were models of brotherhood and promise for the migrating tribes and clans of northern Mexico and the lands of the pueblos. Hope had to be associated with the destiny of people in an often hostile natural environment. For the "native" peoples of middle America, the wandering souls of the Southwest, were a people at war with each other and with the scathing winds of hunger, disease, and change. While the "Christians" who helped to churn those winds were far from the Kingdom of God in their motivations, there were children of the Church who knew how to hold out an honest hand of promise and

and reconciliation. In the memory of the fathers
and lay brothers of the Church lay the image of the
Promised Land that begins with deliverance and
extends its vision to human potential and responsibility. John Tracy Ellis, in commenting on
Crevecoeur's definition of the American, adds: "On
all counts of Crevecoeur's definition except that
of leaving behind his ancient prejudices and
manners, the Catholic immigrant could qualify as
an American. But on that point, one may ask, what
immigrants, Protestant or Catholic, could quality?"
Prejudices, indeed! A heritage of images, a goodly
heritage, more than likely; but a heritage that includes the usual distortions of soul that comprise
the human condition.

Critics who refuse to acknowledge the
saga and its image of the Promised Land usually
demonstrate unconsciously that it is the very power
of that subtle and covert image which has made them
critics of the status quo. And it is also well to
remember that the fullness of the image always has
more truth to be revealed. The Hasidic master,
Rebbe Pinhas of Koretz, is supposed to have said:
"If all men spoke the truth, there would be no
further need to wait for the Messiah; he would have
come long ago." We could paraphrase Pinhas to say,
if all humans lived together in harmony and plenty
with themselves and with nature, we would not
require hope; the Promised Land would be established.
But there is a secret about human existence that
cannot be stated in consistent logic: The Promised
Land is here, and it is yet to be. It is because we
will not accept that truth that we are people without hope, or else a people whose hope lies only in
the conditioned achievements of the shopping mall.

III.

The Promised Land is an image of meaning
for an otherwise abandoned people. In J. D.
Salinger's Franny and Zooey, there is the account
of a disenchanted young woman who has discovered
egocentrism in herself, her lover, her college
professors--everyone is all tied up in some weird
and hypocritical effort to project the self rather

51

than honesty or truth. So Franny determines a course frequently espoused by those who experience such alienation in the self and others. She decides to pursue a way of mysticism which she assumes is meant to transcend the ego and remove her from the phony order of an imposed reality. Like Franny, many of us, old and young alike, have become disillusioned by the hypocrisy of others (although seldom of ourselves) and the phoniness of our nation. And so we have given up on the meaning of our historical peoplehood. We prefer to consider it at best illusory, at worst unworthy.

However, in the novel, it is the role of Franny's brother, Zooey, to remind her of the true meaning of the mystical journey she is pursuing. You had better understand the Jesus you're referring to in that "Jesus Prayer" of Orthodox mystical tradition, says Zooey. It is meant to produce a Christ-consciousness, but that is not the same as picking out your own beautiful Jesus-model (say, a St. Francis) and trying to imagine that the world is like that. It's not the same, says Zooey, as assuming you will avoid the distasteful and ego-centric characteristics of life. Say the prayer, if you want to, continues Zooey, but remember that it is really a prayer witnessing to the need to get on with the work *you can do*. It has to do with accepting reality as the milieu, the context, in which meaning is offered in its own qualified manner. Meaning comes to us; it stands next to us, in relationship to us. That is what we have described as the appositional character of existence.

At this stage of our history, many of us are likely to want to assume the attitude of Franny. We have witnessed the terrors and injustices of the individual and corporate egoes. What is there to do but to deny, by any and all means, the reality of such egoes? They have been the cause of our demise, our disillusion. But there are also those who are the *victims* of the heavy hand of other representatives of egocentric power. They, too, are alienated. Yet it is these people who express their alienation mostly by a desire to claim the material power of their oppressors. In Bernard De

Voto's classical study of the fur trade, <u>Across the Wide Missouri</u>, he writes of the Flathead and Nez Perce Indians who came to St. Louis to learn something of the white man's religion. They came to discover the incantations, the instructions and amulets of the white man's power. If they could acquire those secrets, they could increase their power. And, of course, without knowing it, we taught them in many ways how the secrets of the "white man's medicine" actually worked. If the white man's actions were evil, does that make the actions of the Indian good? The answer is no; both demonstrate a universal and inordinate egoism.

Now, in such a circumstance of alienation, where some of us have been severely victimized by the power of others, where the cynicism and righteous indignation of many lay sullenly across the horizon, why should we not reject all that is in any way associated with the darkness of the day? Like Franny, we may choose to transcend the hypocrisy and the injustice. We have lost the sense of participation in the saga, have begun to deny the worth of the saga. But there is no other existence. And the transcendence that is offered us is meant, as it was for Franny, to provide us with the consciousness that enables acceptance of the saga and our participation in it.

The image of the Promised Land is the only kind of hope that can bring us back into a reconciled existence in the American saga. The image says to those who are abandoned: The promise includes you, too. You, too, must be willing to be liberated from the captivity in which you exist. You must be ready to risk, to transcend, in order that you can be reconciled to the land and all its people. The goal of life is right here "in this world" where we see tragedy and injustice, but it is a goal that is not *of* this world. The image of the Promised Land is one that renews us at the same time that it reconciles us to the saga in which we exist together with nature. The image is of a reality which transforms the world. There are those who continue to say that we must rid our consciousness of all such images. The purpose of their admonition is to make us all face things "as they really are" and get on with task of taking full responsibility for our own existence. But that is to rob us of vision. It is not a new posture at all, as it sometimes assumes. It is one further representation of the assault upon existence that has characterized much of life since the beginning of the modern era. It is misrepresentation of the human journey. It fails to recognize that it, too, is an attitude that derives from images--the image of positivism, for example, that reality is precisely and only as it lends itself to full-scale manipulation; and the image of individualism, that each of us is a sovereign island.

Always before us, the image of the Promised Land keeps us human. It is a radical image that rejects all partial claims to what it means. It reaches into the world, the cosmos, and makes the American saga a reconciliation of the stories of humanity and nature. Those who deny the meaning of the saga by identifying it with some preposterous notion that this nation is in some sense divine and self-sufficient are perhaps even more the cause of the loss of the sense of the saga that those who are repulsed by the extravagances of its meaning. What history means is never lost. The saga's powerful metaphorical narrative of what history means is therefore also not ultimately forgotten. Yet I can hear the hushed breath of Carl Sandburg's "Four Preludes on Playthings of the Wind":

> It has happened before
> Strong men put up a city and got a
>   nation together,
> And paid singers to sing and women
>   to warble: We are the greatest
>   city, the greatest nation,
>   nothing like us ever was.
>
> And while the singers sang
> And the strong men listened
> And paid the singers well
> And felt good about it all,

                there were rats and lizards who listened
                ...and the only listeners left now
                ...are...the...rats...and the lizards.

        It is a bit strange to meditate upon the
fact that either there must be a saga with a vision
of the Promised Land, or else there will be no
history at all. If only the animals--the rats and
the lizards--remain to claim the Promised Land, then
existence has been reduced to the primal chaos.

CHAPTER IV

THE EXPLORATIONS OF PARADISE

What was it that Bronson Alcott said? "...
there, if anywhere, is the second Eden to be planted,
in which the divine seed is to bruise the head of
Evil and restore man to his rightful communion with
God in the Paradise of Good." If the Promised Land
exists as an invitation to the future, then Paradise
is in some way an impressed memory that works its
way through our uneasiness to become an imaginative
recreation of what life is really all about. We can
respond to the promise, to the call of a "not-yet,"
precisely because there is in us the anticipation of
what the promise will lead to. We may idealize the
picture according to the narrowness of our own
desires, imaginations, and expectations. We may see
the "Paradise of Good" with eyes that are veiled by
unsuspected cataracts, or by sight distorted with
the limitations of an insensate mind, but the vision
is nevertheless there. "There are no forms of
disease or corruption, short of death," wrote
Reinhold Niebuhr, "which do not reveal something of
the healthful structure which they have corrupted.
The blind eye is still an eye, though it may be
completely sightless. The aberrations of an insane
mind betray coherences in the very welter of in-
coherences which only a human and not an animal mind
could conceive."

The image of the Promised Land is somehow
connected to the image of Paradise. We discover
that liberation from our present captivity is linked
to a vision of freedom that has already been given
us. We begin to be aware of the fact that the
future that is yet to be given has something to do
with a former wholeness, a prior wellbeing. And so
we bring a new reality into focus that helps us to
understand our world and to deal with it meaningfully.
We envision having to do with "a second Eden," with
a restoration of things as they should be. We see
human relationships and our kinship with nature as
one of "rightful communion with God in the Paradise
of Good." We would probably find it difficult to
go forth on some unknown venture, in search of the

57

Promised Land were it not for the fact that a
recollective image of Paradise keeps us alive.
Paradise is a very important image in the American
saga. If we lose that image we lose our souls.
For there is in the image of Paradise the power to
unite imagination and reason, making transforming
activity possible. Paradise keeps human existence
human. It is an image that brings vitality and
intentionality together in such a way that we
become integrated souls.

If the Hindu were to recall the
"Paradise of Good", he would assume it could have
nothing to do with the reality that is ordinarily
present to us. It can only be found by a union of
atman and Brahmin beyond the illusion of the
present. There are those who expect the visitation
of saviours in flying saucers who will deliver them
from this body of death. The recollection of
Paradise is so intense and their suffering is so
profound that they are drawn to a longing for
escape. Of course, there is always some wistfulness
for escape, some impulse that seeks to drive us from
our present boredom and oppression. No one of us is
ever really free of that incitement. Even that
scientist or technocrat who assumes that he must
reckon only with what is immediately available to
his knowledge and manipulation, has some motivation
to produce that which is "better." And the poli-
tician or revolutionary who believes that only his
own actions will affect any change in the order of
society, is under a mandate to "better" the
circumstances of existence. Yet, how and why are we
so certain that things can be "better"? Do we feel
we have indefatigable evidence to vindicate that
assumption? Is it not rather that the symbol of
Eden, the image of Paradise, has its way with us
whether we will it so or not?

Escape itself is impossible. To be sure,
the Puritan and Jamestown fathers, the agents of
Penn's experiment, and the emigrants from Poland
and Italy, imagined they were escaping the tyranny
of one world, expecting to cool their feverish
brows in the waters of Paradise. Instead, however,
they discovered that Paradise was a wilderness

requiring response and adjustment. The longing for escape is an inevitable human characteristic, a symptom of our continuing dis-ease, our deviation from a basic wholeness. But it is not an *absolute* deviation; otherwise we could manifest no yearning for escape. We are not given the escape we seek, but we are provided with the perspective that is essential for the living of our days.

You will recall, in Aldous Huxley's Brave New World, there was no history, no past, to contend with; and there was likewise no future. The form of conditioning practiced in the society of the "brave new world" was such that a functional present was the only reality. Any inclination to deviate was subdued by doses of soma or some form of suppression of thought. Yet deviation did occur. There were those who found evidence of other possibilities. They sought "escape" from the "brave, new world" (which incidentally, was a presumably happy and carefree mode of being) even if it meant hardship, suffering, or anxiety. In the saga of our existence, the image of Paradise lingers as an incentive for escape that enables a creative adjustment to the actualities of our history.

For some time, we thought of the sermons and songs of the Afro-American as "escapist" sentiment. Militants and intellectuals (black and white) looked with disdain at the paraphernalia of "black religion." There was produced for righteous and sophisticated eyes the portrait of some black preacher lulling his people into a rhythmical euphoria with the sliding cadence of "God's Trombones." He could climb unscaled heights with Moses to promise his tear-stained but smiling auditors that Paradise was theirs in another time and place. Perhaps they had no shoes, never would in this valley of lamentation, but in Paradise they would feel the soft caressing leather of God's own cobbling as they padded proudly along the golden thoroughfares. "Ignorance! Superstition!" pontificated the intellectuals and their vassals, the academicians. "Stupid nonsense!" shouted the militants. "No more of Paradise! Let's get those

59

shoes now--right here!" Now, of course, the militants were much more correct than the intellectuals.
Their strident demands were more indicative of the
actual circumstances of life. For, while the image
of Paradise may have kept some souls of the black
folks in bondage, it also offered *stimulus* for
escape, and for the acquisition of the needs that
had been denied.

    The black preacher and his followers
did not sit idly by waiting for death and Paradise.
They began the laborious journey that had as its
goal the *realization* of something of what Paradise
represented. They educated themselves. They
worked at community organization and mutual
improvement. They began to be a community after
having had familial and tribal relationships
obliterated by the grinding heels of slavery. In
their recollection was the image of a former,
primal well-being. And that image was intensified
by the biblical symbols of a new heaven and a new
earth, and by the recollection of Eden. And even
that militancy which today seeks to deny the
legitimacy of the image of Paradise operates with
spiritual resources derived from the symbol it
assumes is dead.

    The image of Paradise flourished in the
earliest stages of the American saga. Its power
can be traced through the nineteenth century--and
even into the present. Walt Whitman, looking ever
westward, saw it in

          The flashing and golden pageant of
              California
          The sudden and gorgeous drama, the
              sunny and ample lands,

          . . .

          The fields of Nature long prepared and
              fallow, the silent, cyclic
              chemistry,
          The slow and steady ages plodding, the
              unoccupied surface ripening, the

                        60

                    rich ores forming beneath;
          At last the New arrivings, assuming,
          taking possession,...

                    ...

We seem unable to avoid the necessity of the great
symbol. It urges us on at the moment, informing
us that the primitive potential we once encountered
as a people in this virgin land has been treated
rapaciously instead of sagaciously. The longing
for a rich brotherhood of the earth, the sky, and
the common weal--it takes us to mountain retreats,
to communes, to meditation centers. This American
saga--it was to have been a place of restoration,
a place where the races could begin anew. "Most
Elizabethan ideas of America were invested in
visual images of a virgin land," writes Leo Marx.
What sort of terrain would they discover? Well at
one extreme, there was that image of a paradise
regained, says Marx--an image amply retained by
Whitman much later than Elizabethan times. But,
of course, the wild and threatening landscape with
raging storms and strange-looking native inhabitants could lead one to believe that the virgin
land was "a place of hellish darkness." Nevertheless, the very impress of its virgin character was
enough to make it a place where the story of human
potential could be reworked without the frustrations of a decivilizing Europe. Seductive or
foreboding, the image of Paradise was a contributor
of meaning to those who had experienced a growing
inability for what Paul Tillich calls ontic,
spiritual, and moral self-affirmation.

          So Francis Daniel Pastorius, early
resident and leader of the German immigration to
Pennsylvania, could address the posterity, the
"descendants of Germanopolis":

                    ...gather first...
          that your elders and forbears forsook
          Germany, which bore and nourished them,
          in full decision, in order to bring
          forth in this forest-rich Pennsylvania,

                    61

in a wasted wilderness, the remainder
of their lives in the German fashion,
as brothers! (italics mine)

The American Indian may wonder how it can be that
his way of life constituted a wasting of wilderness,
when the way of the white man has severed the very
veins of nature. Yet he, too, lived with an *image*
of what the "Paradise of Good" really meant, and
how he was to live in it. In Edwin Corle's novel
<u>Fig Tree John</u>, Agocho has been travelling for some
time with his wife Kai-a, who is pregnant. They
come upon a spot that was lost in greasewood, with
fresh water nearby and the shade of cottonwood
trees. They decide to stay in this place on the
edge of the Salton Sea. To the vibrant Apache, the
scene was fascinating. "As the sun sank behind the
mountains far to the west and the rapidly changing
light spilled fantastic reds and yellows over the
sky, he stood perfectly still and watched and
listened. And he knew that Na-yen-ez-gan-i, the
War God, was in the sky, and that Tu-ba-dzis-chi-ni,
the Water God, was at his feet, and that Ste-na-
tkih-a, the Chief Goddess of all the Apaches, and
the mother of all fire and water, was everywhere.
Never had he experienced this emotional response to
all the powers at any one time or in any one place.
And he wasn't surprised when he heard the voice of
the Goddess telling him that his wife would bear
him a son in this place, and that the fig trees
would grow, and that the Gods of fire and water
would watch over him and protect him as long as he
remained."

That is an image of Paradise, a portrait
of the restoration of the power of meaning. The
very mention of the gods and the Chief Goddess are
testimony to the fact that the human orientation in
the scheme of reality is not with something which
can be crudely termed "mere nature." Agocho's
Paradise was a desert scene among the cottonwoods.
Pastorius had the lush green mountains and streams
of Pennsylvania to call a "wasted wilderness." It
lay in waste for the German imigrant because it
waited for the gardening of those who had seen
their native Rhineland devastated by Louis XIV of

France. He was somehow aware of that necessity for
the combination of vitality and intentionality that
makes us more than simple participants in the cycle
of nature. The hunting and fishing humans who
darted among the trees and drew their canoes along
the silent eddies of the Delaware River seemed to
the German to allow the wilderness to be wasted.

For both Indian American and white
American the wilderness was understood by means of
an image of Paradise. Each has yet to learn from
the other the real depth and significance of the
meaning of that symbol. The American Indian must
learn the intentional responsibility he bears to
be more than a prisoner of life-process; the rest
of us must learn that our intentionality is always
to be understood in responsible relationship to
the life-process. For many of us, life has become
all intentionality: it is what we will make of it.
But that is because we confuse intentionality (or
will) with the power of the mind. Intention comes
rather from resources deep within us, yet quite
beyond us, that respond only to images--to symbols
like Paradise. The discovery of that truth frees
the mind for appropriate response to life. It is
a first step in producing that reconciliation of
vitality and intentionality that makes us integrated souls.

II.

Paradise is an image of judgment; it
demonstrates the fundamental incongruities of
existence in order that we may improve our world
and live in peace with it. Not long ago, while
driving through the mountains of Pennsylvania, I
came across a scene which can be duplicated
repeatedly in the American landscape. There were
the bewitching, folding shades of green, almost
liquid in their late spring succulence. Each
protrusion seemed to flow in loving promise until
it met the next. Each half-mile of highway
slithered in intimate proximity to this montiform
skyline. Then I rounded a bend in the road,
through one of those gaps made by the joining of
mountain and river. There before me was a peak

63

that was gradually being devoured. It reminded me
of one of the delicious cheese balls my wife pre-
pares for special occasions--golden yellow, rolled
in delicate green herbs. That was it--a cheese
ball, which some giant rodent had secretly discovered! No doubt the yellow sands of that
mountain were essential to the constructions of
what Kenneth Boulding calls "postcivilization"--
that product of science, which is of a "higher
level of organization of human knowledge" than is
civilization, which is "a product of the food
surplus which proceeds from agriculture."

    The purpose of this reflection is no
simple romantic tirade against the terrors of
techno-centrism. At the moment, at any rate, it
is merely to suggest the nature of my response to
that scene. Something inside me was wrenched like
a sudden thrust of indigestive pain. Something had
disrupted the placid and almost unconscious flow of
an appreciative awareness of my surroundings. That
rape of the landscape didn't belong. It was a sign
of dis-ease, of sickness; yet somehow I could understand its necessity *rationally*. There was operative for me the recollection of what the natural
household of humanity should be. The symbol of
Paradise determined my response to that scorning of
nature, just as it would also determine how I would
argue for or against the need for such technological possession of the "things" of the environment.

    When impressionism in painting was born,
human beings were beginning to discover that a work
of art is nothing more than colors, lines, and dots
arranged on a canvas. In a sense they were learning that all art is an impression of reality and
can therefore be done with whatever colors and
forms we choose in relation to our impressions.
When someone says to me, "I prefer realistic works,"
they mean to suggest that they are able to apprehend things as they are in and of themselves. Yet
we know that every suggestion of what something is
in and of itself is already determined by some
symbolic way of dealing with self and environment.
Human beings are more than simple functionaries in
an established order. We create meanings and we

respond to meanings that are greater than our creation or our understanding. And so the artist is correct in insisting that what he creates is equal to what some of the rest of us may require as representational.

The American saga bears in its narrative flow the image of Paradise. It is there to remind us of what the relationships of reality really are in their fundamental character. It is as if we know some secret that was unavailable to us by ordinary ways of knowing and thinking. It is as if something long forgotten by the working memory of the race were operative in us like the instincts of an animal. Paradise judges the cities of man, revealing the thin veneer of "post-civilized" attempts to feign progress. I recently saw for the first time a city which but a few short years ago had been a thriving citadel of middle America. The endless blackened canyons of its great inner core of former vitality reminded me of the decayed muzzle of some bibulous and wasted giant. Its eyes blinded by boarded portals and shattered spectacles, it seemed at times swollen with infection, yet sunken and hollow from a sudden and ruthless malnutrition. Tall red walls and littered, almost empty, alleys. In the humidity of the early summer afternoon, a rancid human fog leaned lazily against the vacant towers. Who could live there? Who should live there? Or work there? The vermin, the roaches, and unwanted humans are left to linger beside the poisoned corpse of the inner city.

And so I ask myself, how is it that I should feel this depressing judgment on the city? Is it not the symbol of Paradise, hidden and revealed in its constant power over our imagination and reason? Without Paradise there is no judgment and no memory of what is real that enables us to risk for the future of a Promised Land. Paradise resides in the American saga as a means of seeing reality in a heavenly manner. Paradise has raised the American consciousness at every moment of our history as a people. Paradise provides an impression of our existence which we proceed to

65

sketch and paint.

Thomas Traherne, in his <u>Centuries of
Meditation</u>, has a beautiful passage illustrating the
manner in which Paradise is an image that brings
reality into consciousness and perspective for us.

> Eternity was manifest in the
> Light of the Day, and *something
> infinite behind everything*
> appeared, which talked with my
> expectation and moved my desire.
> The City *seemed to stand in Eden
> or to be built in Heaven.* The
> streets were mind, and so were
> the sun and moon and stars, and
> all the world was mine; and I
> the only spectator and enjoyer
> of it. I knew no churlish pro-
> prieties, nor bounds nor divi-
> sions; but all proprieties and
> divisions were mine, all treasures
> and the possessors of them. So
> that with much ado I was corrupted,
> and made to learn the dirty
> devices of this world, *which now I
> unlearn, and become, as it were, a
> little child* again that I amy
> enter into the Kingdom of God.
> (italics mine)

What is frequently dismissed as the fanci-
ful madness of a curious "mystic" is nothing more,
or less, than the experience of every man. Traherne
is suggesting that the ordinary circumstances of
existence were seen in a new light, according to a
different perspective. "Eternity was manifest in
the Light of the Day, and something infinite behind
everything appeared..." There are times when we
see and experience only from the midst of the en-
tanglements of self and society, society and nature.
But in such moments, most of our insights and
knowledge are restricted by their immersion in
limiting circumstances and consciousness. However,
there is the occasional vision of Paradise that

helps us to unlearn the restrictive devices of the world, thereby seeing life as it really is--as a child sees it, with the potential of a Kingdom of God, a new Jerusalem, a new heaven and a new earth.

It is that kind of consciousness which sent pioneers on the long hard trek through the Ohio Valley and into the Western plains. It is the kind of consciousness that is re-created in the masked dances and ceremonies of the kachinas; or when the women of the pueblo kneel in their weedy graveyards, offering corn meal baked in corn husks to the Corn Mother, knowing that there is a mystic bond between all that has been and all that is. But it is a consciousness not dissimilar from those American Christian theologians of the nineteenth century, who sought, like Newman Smyth (1843-1925), to break through the particularities of the moment with a fresh image of Paradise: "...though he goes down into the depths, or wanders through realms of strange shadows, and endless confusion, nevertheless, after he has traversed all the spheres into which thought can find entrance, if he remains true to the spirit sent for his guidance, his better self,--like Dante following Beatrice from world to world--he shall find himself at last by the gates of Paradise, walking in a cloud of light, full of all melodious voices."

Peruse, if you will, the so-called "secular" literature of the nineteenth century. Read the papers and addresses of educators and political leaders. Unless you accept the premise that there is such a thing as "mere rhetoric," you will discover there a recurrent version of the symbol of Paradise. Much of the literature of those agricultural societies, whose work led to the establishment of forms of higher education for the agricultural and mechanical classes, to the founding of the land grant movement, has its tone set by the symbol of Paradise. The work of the farmer is lauded, the discoveries of science are praised--all in the context of the paradisiac vision of America and its role in the consciousness of the world.

67

III.

The symbol of Paradise needs to be explored because it offers an image of the garden. And existence outside the garden is a lonely and depraved existence. Why else should we seek to plant the "second Eden," even though we have only faint memories of the first? Henry Nash Smith and Leo Marx have shown how the garden was a profound metaphorical influence on the course of American experience. "When God is about to turn the earth into a Paradise," wrote Jonathan Edwards, explaining the "awakenings" of his day,"he does not begin his work where there is some good growth already, but in a wilderness, where nothing grows, and nothing is to be seen but dry sand and barren rocks; that the light may shine out of darkness, and the world be replenished from emptiness."

Now, of course, there is a dominant Christian tone to this composition of the garden. In an America, influenced culturally and politically by Evangelical Protestantism, we can expect to hear such notes. Nevertheless, there is universality to what they imply. The garden belongs to all humankind. Father John Carroll reported to Rome in 1785, on the state of religion in America. To the Prefect of Propaganda, he suggested that the priests were too few and too old--"almost entirely unfit to undergo the hardships, without which this Vineyard of the Lord cannot be cultivated." To Carroll's Roman Catholicism the garden was primarily the potential place for a harvest of souls for the Church. But his own life and thought suggest that he was aware of the incalculable manner in which America itself was a garden most congenial to what the best of Catholicism anticipated.

The American saga has reminded the Jews who have come into its narrative that the garden is not limited to Protestant labors. Will Herberg has shown that Jewish corporate identity was not lost in America. It may have undergone a change of character, but in such a way that it retained, even enhanced, its Jewishness. There was a time

in our recent history when Jews and Christians,
under the influence of a theological revival and
the rediscovery of religious particularity,
deplored what they called variously, securiza-
tion, Americanization, or religion-in-general.
But a revival of wisdom rather than logic should
enable us to see that every encounter with truth
is always more universal than our particular
appropriation of it. Jewish truth and faith can
indeed be conscious of its particularity, but
it is at the same time evidence of truth and
faith that are universal. "The Jew must become an
American," said Isaac Mayer Wise, "in order to
gain the proud self-consciousness of the free-born
man."

          In this moment of the saga, the memory
of Paradise calls us to a new responsibility. It
becomes extremely wise for us to realize that the
garden *must be, will be,* but that it is to be
shared here and now with the world. Of course, the
American saga has always possessed that wisdom.
But it has frequently been more hidden than
revealed. Then too, it is only possible to
appropriate as much of it as the language and
circumstance of our time permit. It is a wisdom
that is resisted by those who seek to reduce the
truth to their own methods and presuppositions.
W. H. Auden in his Oratorio For the Time Being provides us with an astute vision of its meaning:

               If the muscle can feel repugnance,
                 there is still a false move to be
                 made;
               If the mind can imagine tomorrow,
                 there is still a defeat to
                 remember;
               As long as the self can say "I," it
                 is impossible not to rebel;
               As long as there is an accidental
                 virtue, there is necessary vice;
               And the garden cannot exist, the
                 miracle cannot occur.

For the garden is the only place there
     is, but you will not find it
Until you have looked for it every-
     where and found nowhere that is not
     a desert;
The miracle is the only thing that
     happens, but to you it will not be
     apparent,
Until all events have been studied and
     nothing happens that you cannot
     explain;
And life is the destiny you are bound
     to refuse until you have consented
     to die.

In a very authentic sense, the garden is with us.
The same image that draws us across a continent or
into the hinterland in search of a better order of
time and place must become more than an attempt to
escape. The garden begins to take shape upon the
"dry sands and the barren rocks" when we realize
that there is nowhere else to go, nothing more to
explain. What else but the wisdom of the miracle
of the garden can produce peace and contentment in
the lives of the children of the pueblos, who live
among barren granite walls where the hot sun
presses hard upon adobe walls and makes pale the
scraggily pine and the dusty cottonwood? They know
that "the garden is the only place there is"
because unknown ancestors came up from the earth to
reveal its mystery. And so they return into the
soft folds of the womb to renew its wisdom.

        This is why it is a mistake to assume
that we can reclaim civilization by a romantic
return to the earth. The Indian knows better than
that. And, as Kenneth Boulding tells us, a symptom
of "the disintegration of the city (therefore
civilization) is the enormous rise in this country
of part-time farming." All it represents, says
Boulding, is an "explosion of the city over the
countryside," and the disappearance of a distinctive rural subculture. The garden is at once
pervasive and inspiring, and at the same time
available only in whatever moment we come to terms
with the appositional power of meaning that offers

itself to us. St. John Crevecoeur could say of
America, "Here nature opens her broad lap to
receive the perpetual accession of newcomers, and
to supply them with food. I am sure I cannot be
called a partial American when I say, that the
spectacle afforded by these pleasing scenes must be
more entertaining, and more philosophical than that
which arises from beholding the musty reins of
Rome." And in so doing, he could point to the
gallant figure of the noble farmer responding to
the fertility and growth that awaited his ecstatic
labor. "O what a country will this be at a future
day!" exclaimed one of Crevecoeur's contemporaries.
"What field of delights! What a garden of spices!
What a paradise of pleasure!" But it is for each
generation to learn that the garden is with us,
reminding us of a primordial beauty. The vision of
the garden is important to the American experience.
It is essential and ultimately inescapable. But
its most profound contribution to the affirmation
of self and American peoplehood is the secret
discovery that the "garden is the *only* place there
is," not to be found until search produces only a
desert, until the miracle occurs in which we see
things as they really are rather than according to
our study and expectation. Then it is that we
begin to see the reality of Paradise in the place
where our dreams had fashioned their own greenhouse.

IV.

Liberation, judgment, and an awareness of
the garden are experiences of restoration. Bronson
Alcott, among others, may have been too literal in
his expectations that in this land the second Eden
was to be planted and humanity restored to rightful
communion in the Paradise of Good. Yet restoration
is a necessary human experience. It is not *the
place* that is to be *identified* with restoration; it
is rather that the saga is the accounting of the
continuing realization and enhancement of restoration *in this place*. We can be restored and we can
share our restoration with the world. It is all
part of the saga. Otherwise all is vanity! Many
of us are familiar with Edward Hicks' famous
painting of "The Peaceable Kingdom" (c. 1840-45).

The painting is part of the American phase of 19th century romanticism. But it is nonetheless an important representation of what has been true for the American experience. Colonies were founded, settlements made, communal experiments contracted, cooperative education extended--all in response to the expectation that what had once been true would be restored. The painting is a poetic mingling of animals, children and cherubim against a middle ground of William Penn's peace treaty with the Indians. Here, in this "peaceable Kingdom" the lion would again lie down with the lamb, cease his carnivorous behavior and eat hay like the ox. "The Peaceable Kingdom" is the projected memory of Paradise to be regained, a situation in which existence is restored to wholeness in a very real land of the living.

Many of the 19th century Hudson River school of landscape painters must have had a similar conviction. To observe the lushness of the work of Thomas Cole, Asher Durand, Albert Bierstadt, or Frederic Church is to encounter a revelation of America. Richard McLanathan, commenting on Cole's work, speaks of it as a portrait of what "appeared when untouched by man, of the forces of creation and the expression, therefore, of the Creator. He shared his mystically pious attitude with such of his contemporaries as the novelist James Fenimore Cooper...and the poet William Cullen Bryant..." There was unquestionably present to the minds and souls of many artists, the notion that Adam and Eve were somewhere near, waiting for Americans to enter the arbors of Eden where work was unnecessary, where transparent pools reflected heavy clusters of grapes hanging lustily from the soft shade of reposeful trees.

Americans long for restoration, and they have some understanding of why it is necessary and what is required of them. There may have been an overworking of the power in the symbols of Paradise when thousands of people gathered among the towering oaks and pines for the restoration festivals of the frontier camp

72

meetings. It is not too bizarre to think of the
early 19th century revivals in that light. Nor
is it irreverent or debasing. I have tired to re-
create in my mind those scenes of what took place
in the backwoods of Kentucky and Tennessee.
Historians tell us that the revivalism of the
frontier was greatly influenced by its primitive
setting and soon abandoned the more orderly
patterns of revival it had inherited. And why not?
Not only was the frontier a setting where society
had not yet found its proper structure; it was also
a wild (at times frightening, at times awesome)
kingdom of natural elements, charted only by the
paths of deer and the smokefires of its earliest
migrant inhabitants. In such a world, under these
conditions, it was as true for the white man as it
was for the Indians that fascination, terror, and
awe were the marks of human existence. They
discovered that they were dealing with something
for which there is only one appropriate expression,
mysterium tremendum. It was the feeling described
by Rudolf Otto as that which "*may* burst in sudden
eruption up from the depths of the soul with spasms
and convulsions, or lead to the strangest excite-
ments, to intoxicated frenzy, to transport, and to
ecstacy."

There is little doubt that such was the
similar pattern on the frontier for the white man
and the Red Indian. And there is evidence to
suggest that both peoples acted similarly in the
American wilderness, that they influenced each
other's religious and cultural behavior. Perhaps
not enough investigation has yet gone into the
relationship between the frontier revival and the
American Indian ceremonial and ritual life. Be
all that as it may, it is to my point to suggest
that the primordial image of Paradise makes the
wilderness one of potential and fascination, while
the prior experience of human imagination and
reason in relationship to such a setting produces
fear. In such an intermixtum, such an ambivalence,
we are vaulted into spasm or ecstasy. What is
occurring is a shock to our smugness and the
conceit of our vision of reality. The shock is
the prelude to possible restoration--for imagina-

73

tion and reason. For it is in such dramatic moments that Paradise asserts its power, offers itself to us in the midst of a threatened world.

In our own day, the wilderness has receded; what remains of it has lost much of its power to fascinate and terrorize. We have assumed for too long that it is ours to possess. So how is the need for restoration to be discerned and expressed, for the individual and the nation? The concern for ecology, the attempt to return to a corner of the wilderness, to the small farm--these are more than struggles for survival. They are expressions of the power of meaning in the image of Paradise, still offering itself in apposition to our condition. They are representations of an inner call for a restoration that finds the homogeneity of our postcivilization to be unbearable. What else but restoration is behind the interest in yoga, meditation, and the occult? Something there is that informs us that the world and our experience of it is distorted. In the absence of a pristine wilderness to stimulate our imagination and to bring us to the point of ecstasy, we may perhaps be terrorized by the wilderness of decayed civilization to the point where we are forced into reaction in order to experience the necessity of restored Paradise. At the moment we are something like W.E.B. Du Bois, contemplating the lives of black people, his experience with them as a youthful schoolteacher: "My journey was done, and behind me lay hill and dale, and Life and Death. How shall man measure Progress there where the dark-faced Josie lies? How many heartfuls of sorrow shall balance a bushel of wheat? How hard a thing is life to the lowly, and yet how human and real! And all this life and love and strife and failure,--is it the twilight of nightfall or the flush of some faint-dawning day?"

The answer to Du Bois' question is slow in coming. One thing is certain: that it links the memory of Paradise to a Promised Land; that the past and future are in some mysterious way strangely linked. We *shall be* human because we *have been* human. We shall be a new humanity to the extent

74

that it has been imprinted into the potential of
life, scheduled in the darkness of memory that
began before our consciousness of it. Without
the image of Paradise we shall be less than American, less than human, because the saga that
carries that image also began in the darkness of
a kind of non-history before history.

V.

What of "the machine in the garden"? Can
we rely on anything other than the possible success
of our technologies? "The contest between the
optimists and the pessimists has run its course.
One can prove to the members of our modern
societies that our ancestors never enjoyed this
much means, freedom, happiness, well-being, available opportunities, long life, culture, pleasure,
leisure, communication, and dialogue, but one will
never convince the person in our modern society
that he is living in a little paradise." So writes
Jacques Ellul, in his usually poignant fashion.
But what shall we do? Shall we forget paradise?
Leo Marx suggested in his The Machine in the Garden
that the machine has become so dominant that the
symbols of order and beauty no longer have any
meaning. The images of Paradise and the garden
cannot be embodied in our institutions, says Marx;
all that is left is some "token of individual
survival." Ah, but it is important to remember
that no symbol is ever an individual investment.
It has to do with human *community*, with history
and peoplehood, or else it is nothing more than the
atomistic blossoming of deflowered memory.

Paradise is a master symbol. As such,
it is neither naive trust nor prescriptive policy.
I would not suggest that some childish playing with
Paradise will recover our innocence, make the
machine serve the garden, or evict the accursed
thing from the pastoral landscape. Not at all.
Paradise is not rational explanation or policy. It
is memory, motivation, and expectation. It is a
model for human worth and attainment. It cannot
explain for us what we shall do about the disrup-
tions of our present condition. But its presence

will provide the resource for whatever community
and political realization is latent in the human
drama.

St. Gregory of Sinai put it this way:
"Paradise is of two kinds--of the senses and of the
mind (not limited to thinking power and reason);
that is, the garden of Eden and the paradise of
grace. The garden of Eden is the place where all
kinds of sweet-scented plants have been planted by
God. It is neither entirely incorruptible nor
entirely corruptible. Placed between corruption
and non-corruption, it is forever rich in fruit
and flowers, both ripe and unripe. The trees and
ripe fruit, when they fall, become transformed
into sweet-scented earth, free from the smell of
corruption belonging to trees of this world. This
is due to the abundance of sanctifying grace for
ever flooding the garden of Eden." From that
flooding there enters into the minds of persons the
image they faintly recall, but cannot live without.
The American saga has always borne that symbol and
its appositional power and the saga will reveal yet
other manifestations of it; for the saga is
hospitable, and fuller in meaning than our brief
insights can contain.

We can even hear the Amitabha's description of Western Paradise, sensing that it is a
Buddhist memory at work, contributing its devotion
to our common weal: "and many kinds of rivers
flow along in this world system. There are great
rivers there, one mile broad, and up to fifty
miles broad and twelve miles deep. And all these
rivers flow along calmly; their water is fragrant
with manifold agreeable odours; in them are
bunches of flowers to which various jewels adhere,
and they resound with various sweet sounds...and
nowhere in this world system...does one hear of
anything unwholesome, nowhere of the hindrances,
nowhere of the states of punishment, the states of
woe and the bad destinies, nowhere of suffering...
And that, Ananda, is the reason why this world
system is called the 'Happy Land.' But all this
describes it only in brief, not in detail. One
aeon might well reach its end while one proclaims

the reasons for happiness in the world system (Happy Land), and still one could not come to the end of the reasons for happiness."

That is not escape from reality. It is a recognition of the fact that consciousness flows from inexhaustible springs, that it derives from a reality in which we can only participate responsibly. Life is a saga and the image of Paradise is one of its most effective gifts of meaning.

CHAPTER V

THE DYNAMICS OF COVENANT

The call and expectation of the Promised Land, linked with the dim but persuasive image of Paradise, have significant implications in the character of human relations. The American saga has within it what Bernard Meland has called the "root metaphor" in "the vast unfolding drama of Western history." That metaphor is the Covenant. Perhaps no other symbol in our saga will be subject to as much censure and villification as this one. There are numerous persons of ethnic and racial identity who see the Covenant as the ensign of Anglo-Saxon exclusiveness and repression. Or else they suggest that, while Covenant may be important to Protestants, especially of Puritan progeny, it has no place in their own cultural memory or their doctrinal necessities. But, of course, it is not only dispossessed religious and cultural minorities who are suspicious of the Covenant. It is also those doctrinaire representatives of the political and intellectual liberalism that have emerged as a new form of sectarianism in our midst.

There may have been moments in Western history when the Covenant was a lost image. But it is always recoverable, always has been, always will be. For it is as rudimentary to us as any part of our intellectual and cultural heritage. Unless we deny the entirety of the biblical tradition, we are faced with the symbolic norm of the Covenant. Whether we see ourselves as currently influenced by, or devotees of that tradition, is *somewhat* beside the point. For the point is that individual identity, personal freedom and responsibility all have their beginnings in the Judaic-Christian symbol of the Covenant. And if the consciousness of it, built into the Biblical account, is lost, it will be born anew in a moment of resistance to all forms of determinism—religious, magical, astral, or scientific. If it was a lesser image in the mind of the Middle Ages, it was nevertheless never wholly absent. It is certainly incorrect to understand that period of history as being predominantly

79

concerned with the wrath of God, the suffering of
this world, and ascetic withdrawal or hopeful
delivery to some heavenly regions. Although Henry
Adams may have been too depressed by the dynamo of
American industrial power, he was right to say
that "The twelfth century existed for *joy*...It was
hard to see aspiration in a coal-pit, though it
could be seen in the statuary and glass of
cathedrals. The twelfth century was a zest for
'the fun of life'; its product...was the handwork
of joy and required the judgment of aesthetic
pleasure." Overstated perhaps, but helpful in
asserting the refusal of the middle ages to be
tied to the tyranny of nature or of rationalistic
totalitarianism.

Scholars have begun to unearth the roots
of the Covenant not in some precise, almost
instantaneous, sixteenth century disclosure to
righteous Reformers of the Church, but in much
earlier mystical and humanistically oriented traditions. And, of course, the discovery was of an
ancient heritage. And so, even though we may
observe an increased articulation of the Covenant
in the sixteenth century, particularly among the
progeny of John Calvin, we are in no position to
conclude that it is a symbol belonging only to
Puritans and Anglo-Saxons.

I.

Bernard Meland regards the Covenant
rightly as a "seminal perception of the race,"
embodying "what is primordial in our pyschical
experience." And although it may point up
"peculiarities of Western sensibility and hope
which set its people apart from non-Western
people," yet those peculiarities are *particularities* which break out into more universal
forms. "The Covenant, I would argue," says
Meland, "is formative of our understanding of
justice, and possibly of much that occurred in
the Christian reinterpretation and adaptation
of Roman law." Of course, the Covenant embraces
more than justice and law. It has to do with
the sensibility to a communal ground of reality

that is somehow the depth out of which our
individuality arises, to which it continually
returns. It has to do with a power of meaning
which can be expressed in no other manner than
the symbol of Covenant. Our sociologies and
psychologies deal only with what is available to
the cultural and limited mind of the moment.

My father-in-law is a lover of the birds
called martins. I think it may be because he is
basically a lover of life, who wants to experience
what is below the surface of his desires. He
really wants to soar. At any rate, roses and
martins are part of his passion. In the backyard
of his home is a tall iron pole topped with one of
those magnificent palaces required for housing the
likes of this royal community of birds. One even-
ing early in the summer there occurred a most unusual event. I was not a witness, so I listened
carefully to my father-in-law's description. A
squirrel was making his way through the lush green
grass of a wet spring in Maryland. He had probably
just glided down the trunk of the old maple that
stands next to the garage. Three martins had
spotted him. They were either an advance patrol or
the executive council of the community. At any
rate, there was apparently no doubt about their
responsibility or intention. All three began a
continuous process of swooping down at the crafty
little grey rodent. Like fighter jets they
plummeted. Their purpose, which was successful,
was to drive that squirrel as far away from their
lodge as possible. Squirrels like the eggs the
martins intend to hatch. Squirrels have a way of
traversing telephone wires and electrical cables
to get to where they can leap into the martin
establishment. Sometimes they climb the pole; at
other times they pounce from the limb of a neigh-
boring tree.

The accounting of that experience has
been food for reflection. I have raised in my
mind some of the usual, rather childish, questions
which might be explored by turning to a zoology
text, or a work of ornithology. What instinct
helps the martins to be aware of the approaching

danger? How do they recognize their enemy? What
convinces them of the effectiveness of their
offense? When I described the experience I used
words like responsibility, intention, purpose. And
so I must ask whether those birds *know*--whether
they *have* intention, purpose, responsibility? Or,
is it appropriate to confine the explanation of
their actions to instinct? Perhaps it is safe to
say that the relationship between the martins and
squirrels is one of instinct. Probably the kind of
community manifested by the martins has little of
intention in it--so that whatever community is expressed in their relationship to each other does
not extend beyond their "martinizing." There seems
to be no possibility of it extending to include the
squirrel. That relationship is *established*. There
is one other cause for contemplation, however.
Must I not at least ask whether the kind of relationship that we call community is not somehow
written in the primordial memory of all life?
Perhaps it surfaces at various points along the
schedule of existence so that we may see it in what
we term limited instinctual patterns.

Covenant arises out of a primordial
memory of the communal ground of our relationships.
Human relations are measured by the Covenant. And
the relationship between human and animal is
measured in the same way. The martin cannot extend
its community beyond its martinization, to include
the squirrel. But that may indeed be a distortion
of what was original in reality and intention. It
is, of course, rather facile, perhaps unnecessary,
to point out that the actual picture in human relations is often not very different from that of
the squirrel and the martins. What is essential to
remember, however, is that the symbol of the
Covenant has become explicit enough in the American
saga, so that we have little justification for our
instinctual behavior.

Regardless of what one thinks of the
Genesis accounts of the Hebrew and Christian
Scriptures, or of one's interpretation of them, it
may be helpful to reflect on the implications of
some of thatimagery relating to this matter. It

82

is interesting to observe that the first chapter of Genesis has no reference to Covenant. The twenty-eighth through thirtieth verses established a primordial notion that some contemporary ecologians use as a scapegoat for an explanation of the corruption of environment. The ideas of being fruitful, multiplying, subduing, and having dominion are set forth. We may assume that they have something to do with the fact that it has just been asserted that humanity is imago Dei, image of God.

In other words, humanity is created for something other than its immediate cause-and-effect functioning. There are levels of creation and each level is not sufficient unto itself. Each level points beyond itself in relation to an ultimate. That is why dominion is required of us. However, what follows in Genesis is most interesting. Perhaps it is best to quote: "And God said, 'Behold, I have given you every plant *yielding seed* which is upon the face of the earth, and every tree with seed in its *fruit;* you shall have them for food. And to every beast of the earth, and to every bird of the air, to *everything* creeps on the earth, everything that has the breath of life, *I have given* every *green* plant *for food.*'" (italics mine) *There* is set forth the basic order of relationships, which lurks only in the dim memories of Paradise. There is no distortion in that account. Now, if we turn to the ninth chapter of Genesis, we confront Noah *after the flood.* The flood has occurred because humans have distorted the fundamental relationships (should we, perhaps, put this in present tense?). After the flood, God says something to Noah that is quite different from what he said to humanity in the primal instance. He says "Be fruitful and multiply, and fill the earth. *The fear of you and dread of you* shall be upon every beast of the earth, and upon every bird of the air, upon everything that creeps on the ground and all fish of the sea; into your hand they are delivered. *Every moving thing that lives* shall be food for you..." (9:1-3).

A new order has been established as a
result of the misdirection of humanity. So now a
new way of measuring the order must come forth.
"Behold, I establish my *covenant* with you and your
descendants after you, and with every living
creature that is with you...I establish my covenant
with you, that never again shall all flesh be cut
off by the waters of a flood..." (9:9-11)   If
things were as they had been, there would be no
need for Covenant. *Now* it is Covenant that reamins
as the pattern. It remains as a reminder of the
primordial reality of the communal ground. And we
are left with it. In other words, all existence as
we know it is understood only in terms of Covenant,
which is now the standard by which we are aware of
what ought to be the normative character of life.
Covenant is the reminder of the communal ground and
the promise that it shall be the efficacious mode
by which the present and future are judged.
Earlier we described the appositional character of
reality. Apposition is sensibility to the fact
that we know and are known only in response to the
sets of relationships that offer the power of meaning to us. Covenant is a supreme symbol of that
fact.

        When Walter Lippmann wrote his now-famed
A Preface to Morals in 1929, he proposed a "religion of the spirit" which would "not depend upon
creeds and cosmologies; it has no vested interest
in any particular truth. It is concerned not with
the organization of matter, but with the quality
of human desire." Lippmann was rejecting particularity as an absolute. And while it is true that
the spirit of truth is not identified with creeds,
cosmologies, and particular truths, it is also
essential to recognize that the spirit does very
much depend upon those particularities. We are not
in a primordial state of Paradise. We exist in a
situational setting that confronts us with all that
is available to us *in this moment*. And in that
appositional setting, the "organization of matter"
and the "quality of human desire" are inseparable
realities. The only meaningful option available
to us is sensible appreciation of what it means to
hear: "Behold, I *establish my covenant* with you

and your descendants after you, and with every
living creature with you..." When that sentence
becomes apposite to the celebration of your life,
then the courage to be and to do are present to
you.

II.

I have tried to avoid a strict definition
of Covenant. Yet I'm sure I have fallen victim to
our propensity for structural security at many
points in the discussion thus far. Ultimately, the
saga can only be narrated and its symbols only
described. They are vacuous and abstract nonsense
unless they become in awareness what they are in
fact--appositional. However, it is often helpful
to sketch as many of the contours of a symbol as
seem appropriate to the particularities of this
moment's sensibility.

Covenant is frequently interpreted as
"binding promise." To many it means primarily a
contract, a pact entered into. There is no doubt
about the fact that such is an appropriate connotation. In the lore of Jewish people, there is
constantly present the conviction that "the Lord
gave his word." As a consequence of that assurance,
the Jew frequently sees himself and his people as
having agreed to the terms of the Lord's word. The
Jew gives his word to "the Lord." This very
practical understanding of Covenant is not a casual
thing with the Jew. And it is an aspect of
covenant-meaning which he can contribute to the
American saga. It is missing from our common
religious understanding, and from the piety of
Protestants and Catholics alike. It is a connotation that takes the ultimate meaning of apparently
lesser matters very seriously. In theological
parlance, it is sensitive to the "humanity of God."

If the people give their word and keep
their word, they expect the Lord to keep his word
as well. And Jewish piety will let the Lord know
if he has in any way reneged. There is some
evidence of this in the Psalms, where the poet asks,
"Why dost thou stand afar off, O Lord? Why dost

thou hide thyself in times of trouble?" It is
almost to cry out, Where are you when we need you,
Lord? "Do not deliver the soul of thy dove to the
wild beasts; do not forget the life of the poor for
ever. Have regard for thy covenant; for the dark
places of the land are full of the habitations of
violence." (Psalm 74:19,20)

But it is probably in the writings of the
rabbis of Judaism that this frank spirituality of
the Covenant begins to appear in increasing wisdom.
And the Hasidic masters were well-known for their
honest piety. Eli Wiesel reports Levi-Yitzhak of
Berditchev, crying our during Rosh Hashana services:
"If you prefer the enemy who suffers less than we do,
then let the enemy praise Your glory!" And Israel
of Rizhin one day prayed: "Master of the Universe,
how many years do we know each other? How many
decades? So please permit me to wonder: is this
any way to rule Your world? The time has come for
You to have mercy on Your people! and if You refuse
to listen to me, then tell me: what am I doing here
on this earth of Yours?"

The important element in this attitude to
the Covenant is that it represents an awareness that
all that is is *bound together* relationally. There
may indeed be the ultimate unknown behind all
reality as we know it. But insofar as we have any
hint of the intention and character of that reality
in the present existence, that reality is bound to
us as we are to it. Our existence is in terms of
Covenant. So God is as responsible as we are. The
Covenant has been established and that's where it's
left. It would seem that a recognition of this
truth would contribute a great deal to the de-
sentimentalization of our lives. A challenge to
ultimate reality produces results. It changes the
very contours of thought and existence. The Jew
thrusts that important comprehension of Covenant
into the American saga. And the particularities of
covenant-understanding which we have had are broken
to reveal greater truth.

Along with a frank spirituality rather
than a snivelling or hypocritical sanctimoniousness,

86

this dimension of the symbol will return to our common experience the wisdom of human commitment and promise. "Is he as good as his word?" is a query that really means "Is his word a measure of a goodness that we can trust?" That kind of question is a derivative of the Covenant that has become part of our popular consciousness. We base certain business transactions and political expectations on this common belief. A television commercial bases its credibility to a great extent on this fundamentally religious conviction. If covenant were not the norm, how would any *appeal* to human behavior be made?

Quite early in the American saga we began to demonstrate that this dimension of the Covenant was losing its claim upon us. "Covenants" were entered into with frivolous and questionable intent. We began to be less than the full measure of the word. But, of course, that in itself is to a great extent an indication of the *power and necessity* of Covenant. No human relationship is a complete representation of the fullness of the communal ground that Covenant alludes to. Yet we must hold each other to it.

The conscience of the American Indian wonders at the "forked tongue" of the white man. Cornplanter, Seneca leader, spoke to President George Washington in 1790: "The land we live on, our father received from God, and they transmitted it to us, for our children, and we cannot part with it... Where is the land on which our children and their children after them are to lie down!" The statement was made prior to the making of a treaty-- sacred "as long as the grass shall grow." The United States broke the treaty in 1964; and the grass itself has lost the measure of Covenant due it in the sacred bond. The grass becomes the turgid basin for the waters of our postcivilization. It has been commonplace in recent years to point to the many instances in which the Covenant between white man and red man has been broken. The red American, too, had an understanding of Covenant. It is important not to become overly-sentimental in the way of present-day American liberals who champion

87

every cause in order to be identified with righteousness. The red Indian is not the noble savage, the
primal righteous one, just as he is not the bar-
barian portrayed by many American artists of the
19th century. The work of the artist J. Grasset de
St. Sauveur in the late 1700's depicted the dress of
the Indian with great accuracy, but he succeeded in
painting scenes that symbolized the terror of the
frontier and its fear of the scalping of Indians on
the warpath. Of course, part of that apprehension
was the white man's anxiety in the midst of a dark
and massive wilderness.

There is no doubt that what was at first
the inquisitive and uneasy bartering between
European and the earlier red immigrants turned into
the extinguishing of the latter by greedy developers
of land and resource. The red American was forced
into sometimes ferocious measures of self defense.
But from the first there was also the encounter of
those missionaires of the Roman see, often dedicated
persons who cared only to share God's Covenant and
their own lives-in-covenant with these Indian Americans. Imagine if you can, what it must have been
like for Europeans, whose civilization had endured
through centuries with only occasional contact with
peoples of other cultures, to confront the red man
in the wilderness. Imagine also the reaction of the
simple cultures of the reds to the rather awesome
clothing, equipment, and demeanor of the whites.

We can understand the ambivalent manner
in which the Jesuit Jean de Brebeuf, could say to
his colleagues: "You must have sincere affection
for the Savages--looking upon them as ransomed by
the blood of the Son of God, and as *our brethren*
with whom we are to spend the rest of our lives."
His work had begun among the Hurons as early as
1625 and the repose of the wilderness had already
been stirred up. The mind of the Indian was
sensible primarily to an inner working of nature,
whereby the vitalities of existence determined
thought and will. The sacred trust of the Indian
was confined to the understanding of that power
which was essential to keep one's place in the
order of land and nature. But it resulted in the

clash between tribes whose natural power claims were antagonistic. The so-called "primitive" understanding of reality is an important one, but it assumes that humans exist in an absolute paradise; and the "primitivist" insists he can return to that state.

When the repose of the American wilderness was disturbed by the encounter among tribes and the appearance of the white man, the Indian mind could respond mostly in terms of its own logic. As Edwin Gaustad puts it in A Religious History of America, Jesuits like Brebeuf were caught in the crossfire of that logic and were martyred by it. Father Isaac Jogues was to meet a similar fate when an epidemic broke out near Ontario. "By a primitive logic, (not altogether outgrown in the modern world) the Hurons reasoned that since the plague arrived after the priests had come, the priests were naturally responsible for this unnatural distress. As Huron chiefs deliberated the proper time and the proper means forputting the missionaires to death, the Jesuits, fully aware of the deliberations, continued their faithful ministry to the sick and dying." Jogues experienced one occasion after another in which he was caught in the crossfire of primitive logic and warring tribes. The end finally came during a peace mission when "a Mohawk axe granted him the release of death."

The Covenant is not only a contract, it is a reminder of our constant separation from the communal ground of reality. Contract is necessary because of separation; and no contract is an affair of pure motivation or intent. However, a recognition of that fact itself makes human compacts more effective. For, to paraphrase Reinhold Niebuhr, the other party is not as dishonest as we believe her to be, nor are we as honest as we believe ourselves to be. And what is the measure of justice in any human relationship? The Covenant. We are cognizant of our shabby treatment of the American Indian because we know that a fundamental characteristic of human relations has been abused and corrupted. And if the Indian demands justice for himself in a genuine and profound manner, it will be not only because he wants his due, or wants his power (medicine) returned to him; it will also be because he is mindful of his own distorted participation in a world that is not absolute paradise, that he desires the honesty of human relations to which Covenant points. We may be able to recover the integrity of the human word and agreement when we become conscious of the fact that Covenant is more than simple contract. Contracts can be sealed and unsealed. Covenant is the before and the after of any human compact and it is the measure of their truth and effect.

III.

Covenant declares that chosenness is an appropriate element in the human pilgrimage. There is a universality to the Covenant symbol that has found its expression in numerous and particular moments. The Hebrew Bible begins its story of Covenant with the myth of the flood and the legends of the patriarch Abraham. "And I will make you a great nation, and I will bless you, and make your name great, so that you will be a blessing. I will bless those who bless you, and him who curses you I will curse; *and by you all the families of the earth shall bless themselves*." (Gen. 12:2,3) The chosenness of Abraham's progeny is a derivative of the Covenant; it is not in and of itself the Covenant.

The Covenant itself is a resident of the powerful realm of myth that has its metaphorical roots in the non-time before Abraham and extends itself beyond every horizon of time and space. Because Covenant is the underlying basis of all relationships, it begins its course of realization with a consciousness of individual significance and responsibility. In the individual understanding of it, there can be no manifestation of the "blessedness of all the families (human and animal?) of the earth" unless *I* am aware of the possibility and the necessity. That awareness is what we mean by freedom and conscience. It is a freedom that is immediately responsible to God and man—to the More Than that is always in our midst, calling us to greater community. In fact, since freedom and responsibility are instantly transpersonal, there

90

is no true possibility of insular individualistic appropriation of the meaning of Covenant. As Bernard Meland has shown in Faith and Culture and The Realities of Faith, what we have really meant by sin is the separation of the consciousness of individual significance from its relational character of responsibility. Sin is whatever stifles the ongoing process that Covenant requires.

We are indeed "chosen." If we have no sense of chosenness, we will not likely be cognizant of the potential of meaning in human relations. But if chosenness seeks to remain in separation from its transpersonal trust, it becomes unfaithfulness. In the story of Israel there is the account of the manner in which the intention of Covenant is broken or neglected by the irresponsible assertion of freedom or "chosenness." The prophets and the Psalmists call attention to this brokenness. It is important to realize that behind every brokenness and neglect, the Covenant itself maintains its fundamental power: "Behold, I establish my covenant with you, that never again shall all flesh be cut off..." Chosenness has simply become the embodiment of its own judgment when it is smug, self-satisfied, or vindictive. Alienation, meaninglessness, and violence are the features of chosenness-in-judgment.

The continuing appositional power of Covenant itself means that it leads to ever new efforts at human interpretation and emphasis. Certainly we can see such efforts in the writings of Jeremiah: "Behold, the days are coming, says the Lord, when I will make a new covenant with the house of Israel and the house of Judah, not like the covenant which I made with their fathers when I took them by the hand to bring them out of the land of Egypt, my covenant which they broke..." (Jeremiah 31:31,32). He refers to the action of the Exodus and the giving of the Torah on Mt. Sinai as the manifestation of Covenant which has been standard. But the Exodus-Sinai event is really only a dramatic historical demonstration of the fact that Covenant is basic, that it begins with freedom and chosenness. And so Jeremiah can speak of "a new covenant." The Christian community quite early became convinced

that the constant breaking of the relationship
between freedom and responsibility can only be overcome by God himself. To the Christians, "God was in
Christ reconciling the world to Himself;" which
meant that Covenant is only achieved when we
recognize our constant unfaithfulness and find ourselves driven beyond self to rely in love on the
power of meaning which is appositionally present at
each moment.

When the pueblo child enters the open
womb of the kiva, he descends into the depths of
his origins in the great mother. There he will
learn his individual responsibility and his kinship
with all that is living. He will learn the history
of his people (their chosenness), and the necessity
of full consciousness of participation in the "one
great life." That is an expression of the meaning
of Covenant. All such stories of ultimacy belong to
the saga and only the honest sharing will bring to
light the full meaning of the symbols. The truth of
each episode in the consciousness of the saga must
confront the truth of the other. The stories and
myths of all peoples must be shared. It is their
encounter which assists in the breaking out of
particularity in order to apprehend a more universal
truth. "Chosenness" must always learn the degree
of its unfaithfulness. It must comprehend the manner
in which it has blocked the threshhold, diminished
the horizon of the power of meaning in the Covenant.

Chosenness and particularity are not in
themselves offensive or unjust. They are inevitable
and necessary, as I have suggested earlier. In the
order of historical reality there is no universality
without particularity. Every particular truth must
in some sense be *the* truth. Professor Jacob Neusner,
a Judaic scholar at Brown University, has said, "I
do not believe that we American Jews, all of us
brands plucked from the burning, were kept in life
and out of the Holocaust so that we might apostatize
to the worship of no-gods of materialism or *ethnic-
chauvinism."* (italics mine) Neusner has suggested
that in America Jews are respected *when they are
Jews,* as religious men and women, not when they act
as some form of tribe. "...we need to decide once

92

again that it is worthwhile being a peculiar people with laws different from those of other peoples. And we must cherish those differences, *insofar as they matter*." That Jewish witness to the necessity of chosenness and particularity must indeed be championed. Its radical commitment to the meaning of Covenant is profoundly essential to the American saga itself. From that Jewish realization of the Covenant we are all in some sense enriched.

"The Constitution of the Church" of Vatican II speaks of the "People of God" as the mutual bond in which salvation is meaningful. God "Therefore chose the People of Israel as this People. With it he set up a covenant. Step-by-step he taught this People, making known in its history both himself and the decree of his will and making it holy unto himself. All these things, however, were done by way of preparation and as a figure of that new and perfect covenant...not according to the flesh but in the Spirit. This was to be the new People of God." There are those of us who believe that the *aggiornamento* of the Roman Catholic Church is in great part a result of the encounter of Roman Catholicism with the American saga. The reforms within the Church are directly related to the efforts of those American Catholic prelates like Carroll, Ireland, Keane and Gibbons, who realized that America represented an entirely new experience with which the interpretation of Catholicism had to contend. Orestes Brownson, in his The American Republic, (published in 1866) tried to show that the very existence of our nation was a manifestation of a religious nature, a re-flection of the Catholic principles on which the Church itself was founded. The Civil War had demonstrated that the principle of Catholic unity is triumphant over sectarian tension. The Catholic principle, according to Brownson, excludes no one--there are none who are less than men and without political rights. The American state "conforms to what each holds that is Catholic, that is always and everywhere religion; and what ever is not catholic it leaves, as outside of its province, to live or die, according to his own inherent vitality or want of vitality." The catholic principle, as interpreted by such as Brownson, is one way of stating the meaning of Covenant.

Professor Robert Gordis, another contemporary Jewish scholar, expresses a very similar principle when he says, "one unfailing elixir of Jewish life is Torah...It is the essential genius of Judaism that it takes *the totality of life* for its province. For the Jewish tradition, scholarship and learning, law and literature, music and art, civic defense and public service, social justice and philanthropy, *love of country and of humanity,* all are part of Torah..." (italics mine) Gordis has recognized that "American Jewry is a new experiment." There is little doubt that the American saga itself bears a power of meaning that is hospitable to the particularities of separate traditions, that the saga carries those episodes in rich diversity as part of its unifying and ongoing narrative. Covenant is a symbol that has been partly derived from specific traditions within the saga, but it is also the bearer of meaning that is more primordial, more than the power of any one tradition to describe or comprehend. It is a symbol offered to the whole of humankind in the movement of the American saga.

IV.

Covenant requires action, but it understands the patience of long-suffering. To explain what is meant, I must return to the Genesis accounts which inform us that Covenant is necessary because our present consciousness of reality is removed from its original paradisiac communal ground. This means that when we recognize the demands that Covenant makes upon our thought and behavior, we should also be sensible to the fact that we shall not likely *achieve* the requirements of Covenant in any final or absolute manner. There is always a future possibility for the Covenant, but it defies simple historical realization.

Covenant calls us to do something about the relationships in which we actually exist in this moment--to struggle for the love and justice which

are products of the sommunal ground. But Covenant
also tells us not to expect that we shall be the
embodiment of its fullness. As William Irwin
Thompson points out in At the Edge of History, we
live at the place where time and eternity meet.
That is a place of crucivixion because we cannot
stand wholly outside or wholly within. It is our
pretense at doing one or the other that leads to
the execution of the Son of Man. From the Jew we
learn that the Galut means that a certain Exile from
society always accompanies our call to be daughters
and sons of the Covenant. Our lives are spent in
"waiting"--*active* waiting for the realization of the
Covenant. They are spent in an environment that is
to a great extent illsuited to our perseverance.
"Owning the Covenant" used to be a way of describing
the evangelical Protestant response to the Grace of
God. Owning the Covenant means that we realize fully
that we are children of the saga.

At this moment in our national consciousness, we seem to be the prisoners of time, a kind of
nontime that conveys us round and round a belt of
mechanical birth and death. There is what Mircea
Eliade calls a homogeneity to our circumstance; we
are basically desacralized. But if that is true, it
is not something to celebrate because it will mean
that time and our holiness in time mean nothing. It
will mean that only success can be the measure of
life--lived in terms of annuity funds, insurance
claims, property investments, and increased income.
Only if we have some sense of creative and vital
participation in a saga that bears symbols like
Covenant can we know what it means to have time
sanctified. Time and space get their orientation
and organization from the creative power of meaning
in the Covenant.

In Frank Waters' novel of Indian life,
called The Man Who Killed the Deer, the legal
counsel of the district Indian Service office is
advising the Governor of the tribal council to
forget the actions of a young man who has trans-
gressed Indian tradition. Forget it, says the
counselor, and just enjoy the good things the
government has provided. "They schools, but

95

mebbe soon no children," replies the old man, "They hospital, but mebbe soon people they dead, no sick. They new acequia and maquina, but mebbe soon earth she die too. This Dawn Lake our church. From it come all the good things we get. The mountains our land, Indian land. The Government promised. We no forget. This we say." In the unfolding of the American saga, those who know the power of meaning in the Covenant will always resist the pretense that ignores the communal ground. Justice and truth will be measured in relationship to that ground. This the old tribal governor knew profoundly. To own the Covenant is to repeat, "We no forget. This we say."

CHAPTER VI

UNDERTAKING AN ERRAND

Covenant is the provocation for new beginning. It leads to the kind of activity that has to
do with *effect upon* persons and institutions.
Covenant gives sanction to errand--to mission. It
provides endorsement for the risk and the design
that are essential to the journey in which we are
engaged. We are called to go forth.

Let us try to sketch the contours of the
image of the errand. Certainly, it has been a
prominent motif in the American saga. There are
probably those who would denounce it as imperialistic, patronizing, and paternalistic. To others it
may not be worthy of consideration as a symbol, an
image of significance. But if we accept the notion
of symbol as that metaphorical consciousness that
is evocative of truth and motivation beyond any
particular moment of comprehension or realization,
then we cannot avoid the fact that errand has been
a characteristic feature of our experience as a
people. It may have gotten us into difficulty at
times, but it has frequently given us a course and
direction that derives its meaning from the
intention of the Covenant itself. The question of
whether there can any longer be any worthy
authority in the symbol of errand and mission is
nevertheless one that must be answered in the
affirmative.

I.

Errand is a confession of authority. When
one embarks on a mission, it is because he has
authority to do so. Some person, purpose or both,
is the source of his errand. Something there is
that becomes the *author* of our destiny. Something
there is that lends itself in intention to us.
Something there is that makes us so aware of the
appositional character of reality that we know ourselves to be participants in the authorship of the
narrative course of destiny. Life becomes an errand;
there is a mission we must undertake. We become

97

confessors of authority.

Near my home in Mesa, Arizona, there is a ruin called "Mesa Grande." It is fenced off by "No Trespassing" signs that announce its historical importance to the city and the earlier culture of the state. On one edge is some open desert property. Behind the ruins creeps the infestuous growth of a new development of townhouses. And along the front of the "Mesa Grande" there winds an asphalt roadway dividing it off from the grounds of a large metropolitan hospital complex with its parasitical satellites of commercial therapeutic conveniences. The ruins are ringed and indented with the runways of bicycles and an occasional trail bike. And children scurry about the parched earth of the forbidden territory. My own daughters have come home with shards, collected from some neglected corner under a tumbleweed.

The rolling mounds seem especially small in the midst of an alien civilization. But they have set me to occasional unscientific reverie. Setting aside what anthropologists may have to tell me about them, I have tried to meditate on circumstances. What was it that determined the cessation of activity at the "Mesa Grande"? How did it feel to depart from there, to leave so much remnant of the pulsation of human love and sustenance that it is still possible to kick up evidence in the dust? Was it the urgency of some natural catastrophe-- food, draught? Or, were the people confessors of an authority that sent them on an errand--to a new site for their destiny? I can imagine a people who are so close to the imaginative force of reality that they are uniquely sensible to what they must do. I can appreciate the power of the apposite that would lead them into a strange new venture.

There are many people whose destinies are shaped by errand and mission. Individuals. Groups. Tribes. Clans. Nations. The institutions that facilitate and sometimes control the fate of civilization. There have been errands of mercy and missions of malice. It is perhaps only when the errand is a derivative of the Covenant that it is a

98

true confession of authority. It is then that the
errand is one of freedom and responsibility. It is
then that it points to ultimate "blessing" for all
the peoples of the earth. I can understand that
"errand into the wilderness" of the Puritan fathers
because theirs was to be an experiment in Covenant
for the eyes of the world to see. They were to
implement that model of benevolent human relations
that Europe in its blindness and decay could not
complete. And I can understand, though not condone,
the myopic manner in which the discovery of their
own chosenness kept those Puritan fathers from seeing beyond their own blueprints for the "city upon
a hill." And the degree of judgment that affects
my understanding of those Puritan fathers is a
derivative of Covenant itself.

How desperately we are in need of the
authority of errand today. There seems little
future for humankind; and the American saga flows
on its way, peopled by half-conscious participants
without a sense of mission. Only a sensibility to
a common errand will bring us together as a people
who accept the unique truths that each of us
represents. For example, we cannot do away with
those who will not use our language to champion the
righteousness of our special causes. If the middle
class working man scoffs at the claims and admoni-
tions of the National Organization of Women, there
is nothing to be gained by deciding that the former
are "pigs"--perhaps to be slaughtered. As a matter
of fact, it may very well be that it is only the
rhetoric he will not accept because it threatens
the mode of existence he works so hard to sustain.
He is not really so stupid as to suppose that these
are human beings who are less worthy than he. He
wants only to be certain that he does not lose his
only base of equality and maintenance in the process
of someone else's achievement. And liberation
rhetoric often becomes that kind of threat. It
suggests to the blue collar worker that he thinks
incorrectly, speaks incorrectly. It implies that
his world is unworthy, that he himself is to be
sacrificed in an effort to destroy his world. We
are in the American saga *together*. And if we
concern ourselves *less* with rhetorical demands and

99

proper ideology, and more with our common errand, we shall *discover* rather than *construct* the justice that is the heart of our concern.

II.

Errand is in some sense the result of contemplation and awakening. One does not undertake a mission without careful deliberation, followed by clear and certain conviction. "In service," said Meister Eckhart, "the man gathers the harvest that has been sown in contemplation...God's purpose in contemplation is fruitfulness in works...Saintliness does not come from occupation, it depends upon what one *is*. However sacred a calling may be, it is a calling, without power to sanctify. Rather, as we are, and to the extent that we have Divine being within, we bring blessings to our task."

It is almost a commonplace to point out that Western consciousness has been notably contrived and restricted in recent history. We have not dared to venture out beyond the prescribed warrants of our intellectual orthodoxies. We have lost that cognitive discrimination that realizes we are not what we ought to be or can be. Accordingly there is nothing that motivates us and assists in the development of styles and techniques--what Jacob Needleman calls the "instrumental" character of religion--that alter our personhood in preparation for greater service. "Saintliness does not come from o-cupation, it depends upon what one *is*." But we have been taught that what one is, one is; that what should be sought is a basic adjustment to that fact. The art of contemplation has been much neglected until the "youth" of our culture began to seek altered states of consciousness in the meditational styles of the Orient. We must rediscover that the mind and the hands are the servant of what one *is*. What one *is* requires contemplation as a means of discernment. What one *is* is quite different from what one assumes one is. Contemplation discerns true selfhood and even brings psychological refinement where once madness reigned. Rufus Jones, in his studies of mysticism, has suggested that far from being the flowering of

100

insanity, the contemplation of the "mystics" was
frequently a "cure of souls."

The use of the term "mysticism" may be
unfortunate for this stage of our discussion. What
I am advocating is a rather simple recognition of
the fact that unless we take time to develop per-
spectives on our selfhood, we shall not be free and
effective human beings. Unless we contemplate the
appositional character of our existence, we shall
be custodians of pretense. Unless we reflect upon
the power of meaning in the Covenant, we shall not
enhance the human drama. "I should like to make
every man, woman, and child discontented with myself.
I should like to awaken in them, about their
physical, their intellectual, their moral condition,
that divine discontent which is the parent, first
of upward aspiration and then of self-control,
thought, effort to fulfill that aspiration even in
part. For to be discontented with the divine
discontent, and to be ashamed with the noble shame,
is the very germ and first upgrowth of all virtue."
So wrote the Englishman Charles Kingsley. What is
striking is its similarity to the conscience of the
American saga in the 19th century. Emerson,
Thoreau, and many another American could have
written those same words. It was the sentiment of
many in both orthodox and transcendentalist camps.
It could have been expressed by Catholic, Protestant, and Jew. The village agnostic might have
penned it for the pages of his weekly gazette.
What is ordinarily missing from our understanding
of such words is a certain literal apprehension of
them. To us they have become good sentiment, an
expression of fine and noble opinion. But we do not
expect to enter into any changed state of consciousness and conscience that will send us on an errand.
We prefer to leave it as poesy, not to encounter it
as power.

Huston Smith has described the result of
his first ingestion of mescalin. A phrase--"empiri-
cal metaphysics"--came to him. Previous to this,
emanation ·theory and other characteristics of
Indian cosmology and psychology had been simple

101

academic tools for Smith. Now they became *objects*
of direct, immediate perception. He saw that the
experience he was having *required* the *theories.*
Historians of philosophy had credited such world
views to speculative geniuses. Smith was amused to
learn that those "geniuses" were probably no more
than "reporters." His experience accounted for the
origin of the "philosophies" and supported their
truth. Many of the great philosophical geniuses of
the past may have been primarily reporters of the
vision of truth derived from contemplation. That
may explain why there is little philosophical
"genius" today. Most academic philosophers operate
from the premise that respectable philosophy is
logical and rational thinking in and of itself.
They frequently interpret the "thought" of past
philosophers in completely abstract fashion--with-
out reference to the place of the art of contemplation in virtually every philosophical giant.
Plato, Aristotle, and Plotinus are obvious representatives of the art of contemplation. But we
can include Spinoza, Descartes, Kant, and Hegel,
as well as many others. Creative philosophy is
the effective reporting of contemplation. And the
reporting of a cobbler like Jacob Boehme or an
Indian shaman may be of equal value to the work
of the "respectable" philosopher or theologian.

        Contemplation is not planning or design.
It is preparedness to receive. It is openness to
the appositional reality that offers power of meaning to us. From the folk tales of the mountain
people of North Carolina and Southwestern Virginia,
Richard Chase has gathered a collection entitled
Grandfather's Tales. One of them is called "Soap,
Soap, Soap." I have read it over and over to my
children. They have laughed and laughed at the
humorous situation and the rhythms of sequence
that are part of the folk tale. Only as I write
these words has it occurred to me that the story
is a very unpretentious illustration of the truth
under discussion.

        I cannot recount for you the whole tale;
and you will certainly miss its humor and simple
beauty. But let me try to describe the situation.

A small boy, dressed in the tattered clothes of the rural poor, is told by his mother to go to the village general store to buy her some soap. The lad goes skipping along the dusty road, mumbling "Soap, soap, soap" in order not to forget the purpose of his junket. In fairly rapid sequence he encounters adults whose questions or plights interrupt his need to continue repeating, "Soap, soap, soap!" After the very first interruption, he has had his memory jumbled, and the boy goes on his way, repeating the words, "One's out; get the other'n out--one's out, get the other'n out." That's because he has just been whipped by a man whose wagon was mired with the wheel in a mudhole, and forced to help get that wheel out. It has now been some time since he remembered the errand of the soap. And, of course, he soon comes upon a one-eyed man who takes great offense at this latest chant.

The misfortunes of the poor lad multiply until finally his crying arouses pity in a woman who tells him, "You run on back home and tell your mommy to take some *soap* and wash that dirty face." Only the irruption of the original word "Soap" into his muddled consciousness awakens him to the purpose of the trip he has been taking in aimless fashion.

Wandering consciousness! Engaged only in the concentration of each segment of our journey, far removed from the mission of our destiny--until that moment of awakening which lifts us above the quotidian. For the country lad it was not contemplation that made way for the discernment of his errand, but the resultant awakening was much the same. For many of us, contemplation is the only way. It is that concentration on the Covenant which takes us beyond what it ordinarily means to our meagre understanding. The awakening is not the *product of* the contemplation; it is the gift that comes when contemplation takes us as far as the mind and the imagination can go.

Errand proceeds *from* community on behalf
of community. One assumes responsibility for a
mission because his relationships with others and
"the other" have produced a community of meaning
which must be shared. He undertakes an errand out
of the midst of the experience of community in
order to bring into existence another manifestation of the same meaningful community.

The Evangelical Protestants of the East
Coast in the first third of the nineteenth century
were a community. The scope of that community was
more universal than the particular forms of its
variety of institutional families. There is no
such thing as an "Evangelical Protestant," by way
of institutional or other formal identification.
Yet the term is an extremely significant one, with
a number of distinguishing features which
historians like Sidney Mead have labored long to
interpret. It included a diversity of denominations, and was even greater than the voluntary
associations of Christians who had experienced
conversions and sought to express their new life
in terms of service on behalf of an improved
American society.

That innumerable company, with its
diverse sub-communities, was very much concerned
about its "errand into the wilderness" of the
expanding Western frontier. And well they might
have been concerned. For, human community does
not come easily. The frontier settlements were
frequently the stations for the most debasing
forms of behavior. The civilized "Protestant"
culture of the East was concerned that the
barbarism of the frontier would threaten the very
destiny of the nation. They were deeply concerned
that the people of the Western wilderness should
know what community meant. To that end they were
also concerned to send their mission from the
churches and societies of the East to enlist the
settlers in the civilizing, community-affecting,
responsibilities of humankind. To save souls, to
establish Christian churches was to bring community

and civilization to the disorderly frontier.

There is a tale from the Sufi tradition that bears on this point. It seems that the Mulla Nasrudin was invited to address the citizenry of a certain village. He stood on the platform before the assembly and asked, "O people, do you know what I am about to tell you?"

Some hecklers in the crowd, thinking to have their usual amusement on such occasions, shouted out, "No!"

"In that case," said Nasrudin with unruffled composure, "I shall not attempt to instruct such an ignorant community."

Sometime later, the elders of the village convinced the Mulla that the ruffians would not bother him if he would come again to address their people.

"O people!" said Nasrudin from the rostrum; "do you know what I am about to say to you?"

Of course, there was a bit of uncertainty, how to respond. The people were somewhat intimidated by the piercing stare of the Sufi teacher. They muttered, "Yes."

"In that event," exclaimed the Mulla, "I have nothing more to say to you." He left the assembly.

On the third occasion, after the elders had appealed to the teacher to make one more attempt, he stood before the people and began "O people! Do you know what I am about to tell you?"

What was there to do? A reply was necessary. So the villagers shouted, "Some of us do, and some of us do not."

"In that case," replied Nasrudin as he left the hall, "let those who know tell those who do not."

That tale, like most such accounts, lends itself to a variety of levels of encounter and interpretation. Indries Shah suggests that it means "if there are some enlightened people in a community, there is no need for a new teacher."

There is no errand that does not proceed *from* community *to* community. To the extent that community is absent from our twentieth century existence we shall probably also be unaware of the errand that is essential to creative human well-being. Robbed of a sense of mission, we have little that continues to hold us together as a people, to provide us with the experience of "coming out" and "going forth" which is so essential to purposeful living. The problem is circular. For, there is no mission that does not itself arise from community. Mission does not have to issue out of paternalistic, triumphalistic, or defensive motivations. R. Pierce Beaver's Church State, and the American Indians offers a significant insight into the missionary posture of the American denominations in their relations with the Indian Americans. There had always been present the notion that the red man was a heathen requiring conversion to Christianity. But that attitude must be represented in relation to a European history which understood civilization to be marked by the contours of the Christian Faith. Therefore, any contact with alien culture required a mission of conversion that included the embrace of civilization. Now, in the eyes of some, that may not be justified. Nevertheless, it is an explanation of one type of missionary attitude that occurs not only in American and European history, but also in other situations where some form of enlightenment brings its devotees into contact with a foreign people. The movement of Buddhism into China, Tibet, and then Japan had a distinctive missionary character to it. It sought to share its enlightenment with those who still lived in darkness. And the sharing was not always patterned after the ideal of the bodhisattva.

American churches looked to the Indian on this continent as a people in darkness requir-

106

ing light. But they sought to educate, and in many
cases opposed the removal of the Indians to frontier reservations. Frequently, as in the case of
the Moravians in Pennsylvania, there were those who
were successful in establishing Christian *communities* of Indians, even of whites and Indians together. It was political manipulation which
destroyed the peace those Christian communities had
effected. Now, it is not my purpose here to argue
for the righteousness of Christian missionary
activity among the American Indians. What I am
suggesting is that any discovery of community that
is not just instinctive, or according to nature, is
bound to produce a mandate, an errand. The
resulting mission may be one of paradigm--demon-
strating the model with the possibility that others
might adopt it. Or it may be one of active
persuasion. In either case the goal is a transformation. And there is no escaping the varieties of
human motivation that may enter the picture. Anyone who feels she is in possession of truth or
power can become quite patronizing of others--
witness any "discussion" among academicians at a
dinner party. At tea time "To and fro the ladies
go, talking of Michelangelo." We cannot avoid
entirely our feelings of superiority, of triumph
over others, of fear that others may threaten our
own truth and its security. Such attitudes and
unconscious feelings may *qualify* our errand, but
they do not *eradicate* the real potential for
meaningful community.

The Puritan fathers, the Palatine
immigrants, the Franciscan saints were all on an
errand. And the Slovaks and Italians who arrived
on our shores could well envision themselves as a
people setting out to accomplish what they had
been unable to achieve before--because America
itself was on an errand. The saga is slow in unfolding the dimensions of mission which we all
share. Partly that is due to the amnesia in which
our culture currently moves. The insensate manner
in which we have become functional victims of our
ability to convert nature into resourceful gain
and to construct the rudiments of our own consciousness is little short of death itself. If

107

there is no errand, we come from nowhere and we go
nowhere; our songs and our recreation are the
festivities of a mourning band plodding across the
flatlands of meaninglessness.

Some time ago I revisited the place in
Pennsylvania where I had lived for ten years
prior to moving to Arizona. My visit was not a
short one. It was of several weeks duration and
I had opportunity to visit with many old friends
and acquaintances. But the irruption of wonder
occurred one day as I was walking along one of the
main thoroughfares of the downtown area. I saw
familiar faces, but it seemed as though they were
out of place. I wanted to place them in another
town--perhaps in my present home. The faces and
voices belonged with me in a community of meaning
that had no geographical limitation. There were
the greetings of those who were surprised to see
me and there were the absent-minded "helloes" of
those who were seemingly unaware of an absence of
several years.

My reflection accompanied me to the
home of a friend where I was staying during my
visit. I looked out the back door to the tall
oaks and elms that bordered the park. I took in
the bushes, the cardinal who sat majestically on
the crab apple tree. As my eyes met the grass,
with its clotted rows of brown castings from a
recent mowing, I felt a brief thrill of oneness
with--what?--life, the universe? I can't say! The
only thought that came to mind was, "How is it
possible to be so many places at once? How can my
consciousness touch this house, this lush green
summer in Pennsylvania, the lives and loves of
people who live in this place and also other
houses, other faces and people who are many miles
away?"

I don't know at this moment whether I
have put into words what I have felt. I only know
that to me it is a miracle, a display of magic
that no explanation satisfies. It is the surprise
of community--with people, with all of life. It
is a surprise that cannot die, because community

cannot die. As long as such surprises are possible
I am both a free human being and an agent of
community. I am a person on a mission. And I can
understand the deep stirrings that caused John
Winthrop to say, "we must delight in each other,
make others' conditions our own, rejoice together,
mourn together, labor and suffer together; always
having before our eyes our commission and community
in the work, our community as members of the same
body...we shall find that the God of Israel is
among us...he shall be able to make us a praise and
glory, that men shall say of succeeding plantations:
the lord make it like that of New England..." That
errand is still ours; it belongs to every American
as he contemplates his own unique role in the saga.
Our blackness, or redness, our ethnicity, may
justify for us a special degree of chosenness; but
it does not eliminate the errand we must take from
community to community, in order that life together
may be enriched and enhanced.

IV.

Errand has to do with the *quality* of life.
The image speaks of a basic human desire to amelio-
rate, to improve, to better the character of
existence. The image was translated into the American experience very early by the biblical imagination of Christians. It drew support from the
European longing for a Promised Land, where
Covenant would be the recognized heart of the
future. The Puritan "errand into the wilderness"
sought to carry the qualitative existence represented by the Covenant into an otherwise chaotic
environment. It was a mission to provide spiritual
order. Such missions may sometimes prove abortive
or violent. That is the result of the human condition, and in no way relieves us from the necessity
of involvement in the errand on behalf of qualitative existence.

Much of what Walter Lippmann had to say in
A Preface to Morals is subject to sharp critical
review. Yet there are still moments of prophetic
vision to be experienced from his manifesto of 1929.
The religion of the spirit, says Lippmann, "can

endure the vanity and complexity of things...It
seeks excellence wherever it may appear, and
finds it in anything which is inwardly understood;
its motive is not acquisition but sympathy." I
have some reservations to bring to the notion of
"inward understanding," since I believe that it is
in *outward* understanding that we are most true to
ourselves. It is at the *horizons* that we encounter
the appositional powers that offer us meaning and
motivation. The metaphor of inwardness usually
leads to the exclusion of what is outside. What
is not inside then becomes "secular." But the
outward movement to the powers of apposition
always *includes* what is inside; it has no
tendency to suggest that what is inside is not
sacred. For sacredness is consciousness of
meaningful relationship to the universe. Nevertheless, Lippmann's call for response to excellence is
an important dimension of what the errand requires.
He tells us: "The ordinary man believes that he
will be blessed if he is virtuous, and therefore
virtue seems to him a price he pays now for a
blessedness he will some day enjoy." But virtue
itself is a dull put-off; its rewards seem deferred,
vague and doubtful. In the realm of what Lippmann
calls the spirit, however, "there is no future
which is more auspicious than the present... Evil
is to be overcome and happiness is to be achieved
now, for the kingdom of God is within you [the
kingdom is "among" or "in the midst of", conforming
more accurately to the true pattern of experience].
The life of the spirit...is a kind of experience
which is *inherently* profitable." One undertakes an
errand on behalf of such an experience as that.

    Charles M. Schulz's cartoon books remind
us that "Happiness is a warm puppy;" "Happiness is
walking in the grass in your bare feet;" "Happiness
is three friends in a sandbox...with no fighting."
In one of Schulz's little comic sketches Linus is
seated on the floor, his portable radio next to him.
His mouth is crinkled and turned down, his brow is
furrowed, and his eyes droop in their tiny sets
beside his button nose. The caption reads, "Happiness is a sad song." That "sympathetic" turn of

110

mind includes an acceptance of the moment, but also probes the secret joy of being able to empathize with sadness. Oh, to be sure, it may border on the sentimentality we have struggled so laboriously to debunk. But sentiment that is aware of its dangers is essential to the warmth of human experience. I am one who had trained myself to avoid sentimentality. Yet I have often been surprised by it. Recently I saw two athletes--one black, one white--embrace each other after a relay race. There was a lump in my throat and a tear in my eye (literally). I had not anticipated that response, therefore I had no defense against it. And I couldn't help thinking, that's the way it *has* to be; there is no alternative, but death.

The errand has to do with the quality of the moment. It has to do with a happiness that demands holiness. Not just dedication. Not merely the drab pursuit of virtue that makes sadness itself a work for future reward. Instead sorrow and joy are themselves moments in the contemplation of happiness. Holiness suggests the discipline that is essential to wholeness, well-being. Holiness is thought, intention, and action all resolute and unified in their attempt to be the best possible response to living. What one thinks, wills, and feels, and does must somehow be prepared for whatever the moment demands. And so a certain admonition is always necessary. Some word must always call us to account. There must be a trumpet with no uncertain sound, a discipline to which we subject ourselves.

Errand is essentially the extension of the Covenant into the future and among other peoples. However, it is necessary to emphasize that something qualitative is involved in the mission. There is a contrast to be found in the attitudes and literature of the New England Puritans and the German Pietists of Pennsylvania. Both were concerned with this world, but the Puritan expected much less of it than the Pietists. The poetry of Michael Wigglesworth, for example, is in a strident tone. It is harsh in its words and its imagery. The poetry of the

Pietists also speaks of judgment, but among the
Pennsylvania Germans, it was a warm and imaginative
verse--concerned with the transformation of the
world. They wrote lines in vivid imagery, speaking
of the manner in which wisdom and love become the
mode of our happiness when we share in Christ's new
creation. Puritan and Pietist are both concerned
about the world, but the former was more rational-
istically inclined. He was forced by logic and
systematic thought to be consistent, to revert to
his first principle of God's predestining grace,
thence to despair of the world. But the Pietist
was a person of love, who had known suffering and
discerned wisdom.

V.

Errand is prepared for sacrifice. As
Robert Bellah and the interpreters of "civil
religion" have insisted, the rhetoric of American
experience resonates with the call to sacrificial
duty. The well-known phrase of President John F.
Kennedy is now almost a hackneyed diction: "Ask
not what your country can do for you, ask what
you can do for your country." We do not really
know whether twentieth century Americans comprehend
the meaning of sacrifice. We do not know whether
we are capable of it. Yet we seem to understand
from some great depths that Americans should always
be "ready for the sacrifice" required of them.

However, there has been very little
receptivity to the rhetoric of sacrifice recently.
The response has been a nod of the head that casts
a wary eye sideways to see whether the neighbor is
about to do his share. Only *enforced* speed
limits made a difference on the highway. And, by
and large, the thermostat was turned down because
"others were doing it," or simply because there
was little fuel to be bought. To be sure, there
is a residue of sacrificial appeal still remaining
in the soul of America. But the American soul has
been shaken, its integrity almost shattered. We
have lost the appositional sense of our participation in the saga. The result is that there is
little meaning to our personal existence other than

survival or acquisition. If there is no saga, there
is no Covenant, and no errand or mission to share.
Therefore, there will be no sacrifice. President
Johnson's message to Congress of March 15, 1965,
calling for a strong civil rights bill, stands as a
beautiful paradigm of the invocation to sacrifice.
It is worth quoting here, from Bellah's use of it
in his "Civil Religion in America":

> Rarely are we met with the
> challenge, not to our growth
> or abundance, or our welfare
> or our security--but rather
> to the values and purposes
> and the meaning of our
> beloved nation.
>
> The issue of equal rights for
> American Negroes is such an
> issue and should we defeat
> every enemy, and should we
> double our wealth and conquer
> the stars and still be unequal
> to this issue, then we will
> have failed as a people and as
> a nation. For with a country
> as with a person, "What is a
> man profited, if he shall gain
> the whole world, and lose his
> own soul?"
>
> . . .
>
> above the pyramid on the great
> seal of the United States it
> says in Latin, "God has
> favored our undertaking."
>
> God will not favor everything
> that we do. It is rather our
> duty to divine his will.

Today there are those who would give lip
service, others who would scoff, and a few who would
respond affirmatively to that appeal of President
Johnson's. In a way, it contains a strangely

prophetic note: "For with a country as with a person, 'What is a man profited if he shall gain the whole world, and lose his own soul?'" It is our loss of soul that accounts for our present paralysis, our frustration in the face of political, economic, and environmental tensions at home and abroad. The "righeous ones" understood Watergate as the heartless, unethical machination of evil persons. But the whole episode was such a masquerade of fumble, folly, and expediency that it should be plain for all to see that the issue falls at the feet of doctrinaire and permissive liberals as well as before the veiled faces of those caught performing the very acts which are the *daily unmasked* rituals of business, education, and industry.

The Latter-day Saints have built a world religion on the foundations of errand derived from the American saga. Whether we are adherents of their claims or not, we can observe the success of their mission and certain advantageous results in their community life. It is the duty of the Latter-day Saint to assist in the "work of gathering the saints from the nations of the earth." The Saints' sense of responsibility often takes the form of moralism and ideology, but it also relies upon the Mormon version of the story of America. And while they may have a 19th century expectation of success as reward for the meritorious character of their lives, they are prepared to accept the specific sacrifices that their church and their country require of them.

In similar fashion the Pennsylvania German farmers frequently sacrificed their own well-being for the good of their animals and their land. Their mission was to bring the wisdom of God's Love into transforming relationship to their own lives and to the lives of others of the creatures of God's universe. Their poetry spoke with images of the lily, the turtledove, of the Virgin Sophia, of the Bridegroom and the love which overcomes suffering and brings redemption into the world's folly.

The need to know that we are dispatched, engaged, commissioned--that is basic to our human-ness. But we live today with weak surrogates for our mission. Some cause of justice, severed from the greater Covenant to which we all belong, sends us reeling and coursing into the no-person's-land of twilight warfare. Some expectation of material plenitude or distinction produces its temporary incentive and insanity. Even our urgent crusades for cures and improved health appear as vacant stares on the death-mask of survival. Unless we are a people on an errand, living in the midst of the saga, we shall be an erratic nation of ersatz humanity.

CHAPTER VII

THE BIRTH OF THE NEW HUMANITY

Alice, in Wonderland, has just been thrown the Duchess' "baby," only to discover "...it was neither more nor less than a pig..." Having set the little creature down, she watched it trot quietly into the wood. "If it had grown up," said Alice to herself, "it would have made a dreadfully ugly child: but it makes rather a handsome pig, I think." And Alice began to think about some children she know who might do quite well as pigs, "if one knew," she thought, "the right way to change them--."

There is a certain growing up we humans do that makes for dreadful ugliness in the result. There are times when it seems to some of us that we could accept the character and appearance of another person if only we did not have to consider that individual has a human being. Some crippled confusion in the order of nature suggests itself to us. Of course, in Alice's case, she had really been the handler of a pig in a blanket. It was all very well for her to set it free to wallow in the wood. But there is a strange quirk about our rather ordinary behavior that is frequently only willing to see a pig where a human being actually exists. Perhaps it is only the innocence of Alice in the seemingly distorted simplicity of Wonderland that is really capable of sorting out true humanity. For the rest of us, it may be that we see the "dreadful ugliness" of the other because it is somewhat a reflection of our own pigification. Perhaps some radical experience of Wonderland is essential to seeing humanity as it really is, and to understanding its potential for change, for new birth and renewed possibility for good.

In the American saga there has always been a pervasive measure of wonderland. We have seen it in the images of Paradise and Promised Land. Wonderland is a childlike capacity for seeing through the orthodoxies of reality that are forced upon us by our sciences and cultural norms. The

wonderland in the American saga helps us to believe
that it is possible for a "new humanity" to emerge.
In the telling of the saga, there have been those
who have assumed that mere existence in the lushness of the New Eden made us into Adam and Eve.
But somehow, our innocence is not to be found in
the America of recorded economics, politics, and
geography. For, the points at which the saga
moves from metaphor to touch the ground of actual
human demeanor usually reveal the "dreadful ugliness" of our condition.

Our experience has taught us that being
American means to be sufficiently aware of the new
humanity in the saga--humanity on a new journey
into the Promised Land--so that we might take those
steps essential to change. Change is possible,
said the revivalist. The soul may be given the
grace it needs, said the Jesuit father. The Torah
is the way that directs the life of the chosen
people, was the assurance of the rabbi; it is also
teshuvah, a turning around, a change.

All in all, we are indeed already a new
humanity even though we have been slow to recognize
it. We are the members of a new people which
includes a very rich diversity of peoplehood. There
is a sense in which the tension between wonderland
and the world "above the rabbit-hole" can help us
to accept ourselves and others *as we are*. Not
because *as we are* is "okay," but because change is
possible, in relation to an ever-greater human
realization than the present permits. We are always
more human than we recognize or acknowledge. That
is the story of America. It is already a new thing
to know that transformation is not an elite venture,
but a free and actual reality. No need to assume
that some are pigs, rather than humans; because if
they are truly pigs, then there is no course open
but to let them wallow as pigs do. But if they are
humans, their *apparent* "pigliness" is a distortion
both in your seeing and in their demeanor. New
humanity is a reality; its symbolic power flows
through the American saga.

Many accounts have been written of the
"new world" and its "new man." From St. John de
Crevecoeur on we have moved by day and by night
under the protection and illumination of a rare
configuration of our own humanity. "The Americans
were once scattered all over Europe..." said
Crevecoeur. In and of itself that is a somewhat
ludicrous characterization. Obviously, there were
no "Americans" in Europe prior to the settlement
of this hemisphere. "The American is a new man..."
--he is not to be measured by nationality. What,
indeed, is new about a humanity that merely trans-
fers its residence from one continent to another?
What is new other than the pristine landscape? But
the curious mating of Paradise and wanderer gave
birth to an image of humanity not limited by former
portrayals.

"The American is a new man..." meant not
that citizenship within this wilderness was an
imperialistic distinction justifying condescension
toward the rest of the world's citizenships. It
meant that what was being born here was a symbol of
the transformation of humanity, that a paradigm
belonging to the hopes of the world was taking
shape. Only the extremely shortsighted glimpses of
this image can make us into self-righteous snobs
and pious international poachers. That the latter
has often been the case is no doubt true. But it
is likewise true that the American image has also
had its way with the formation of many of the
world's dreams and principles. Forever open to the
new, the American "must therefore entertain new
ideas and form new opinions...This is an American."

"Few other nations," writes Michael Novak,
"are to so great an extent a creation of consciousness." I would only add, that it is a consciousness not limited to the contours of nationality or
ethnicity. We have so little experience with the
implications of that fact. We are only beginning
to see greater dimensions to the symbol of the new
humanity. The power of meaning begins to break
through the particularities in which it has been
held. The American saga has been formed on the
continent of North America, but it *belongs*

119

ultimately to no continent, no nation.

Perhaps, as the historians of religion might suggest, some form of death must take place before new birth really occurs. We are the constant witnesses of both in our institutions and philosophical constructions. Even our technological accomplishments fall into grave after grave, often of their own excavation. Each success brings an attendant expectation that the "answer" to life's problems has been found. Test tube conception becomes a ritual reenactment of the secret of the universe; and there will be strange new deaths to demonstrate that even these solutions are finite.

It is not within our power to bring about an ultimate resolution of existence. To presume to do so is to perform the ancient and dangerous rites of the alchemist--to become master of nature, to create the homunculus, and stop the movement of time. There is nothing essentially new in such goings on. They belong to the old humanity, but they are misguided, producing a death which gives no rebirth. For, to be completely in control of the universe means that nothing stands outside of that control and we become the hapless victims of our own zombied existence. The death of our self-centered desires should alert us to the fact that something new waits to be born among us. We should prepare to give up the trite, old alchemistical maneuvers. We should begin to ask what kind of new humanity is ready to emerge among a people distinguished by diversity. The new birth will be a discovery that otherness is the measure of all reality--that the neighbor is our selves. We should be tired of the old humanity and become the "last, best, hope of earth."

The American saga is fundamentally the constant symbolic presence of a social mind--an integrated soul that receives its meaning from beyond the crass expectations of the moment or the stifling manipulations of nature. Loren Eiseley puts it this way: "the need is not really for more brains, the need is now for a gentler, a more tolerant people than those who won for us

120

against the ice, the tiger, and the bear." But the
humanity that gave us these latter winnings must
die; and it is fitting that the land that has
demonstrated some of the most audacious of the
feats of that old humanity should be the site of
its death. For the American saga itself has
carried the image of a new humanity which was not
to be confined to winning against "the ice, the
tiger, and the bear."

II.

The American is indeed a new human.
There is none like us, for we are Hopi and Navajo,
Jew, Buddhist, and Christian. We are Cuban, German,
French, English, Armenian, and Japanese. And we
are bound together in the common destiny of one
political realm. The character of our new humanity
is a celebration of otherness. We still retain all
the attributes that made Christian theologians
speak of original sin and Jewish sages reflect upon
the evil impulse. What was described as the fall
of humanity and the doctrine of redemption still
applies to our condition. But there is indeed
something new. For those old doctrines were born
out of the thought patterns and the language of the
old humanity. The truth behind them is greater
than the language contains.

We are a symbolic people and we have
begun to be sensible to the fact that symbols like
God are born out of a less differentiated reality--
what the mystics called Godhead. Godhead is prior
to gender; gender is before sexual separation.
When the Genesis account of the Hebrew Bible speaks
of creation, it represents God as saying, "Let us
make *man* in *our* image..." There have been many
historical, linguistic, and metaphysical attempts
to deal with the wisdom in that statement. But
certainly the immediate truth of it is clear: what
God is, is initially undifferentiated potential
that includes all possibility. The action of
creation begins differentiation--especially with
regard to humanity. Our sexuality is an expression
of the fact that in a new humanity the "other" is
always already part of us. Sexuality is a reaching

121

out and a response. When it becomes less, it is
self-aggrandizement and belongs to the old humanity.
We begin to "use" sexuality. It becomes a "tool,"
a "skill" for manipulative purposes. It becomes
the means whereby our self-centeredness masquerades
as the whole of human reality. The irony of this
activity is that it reduces us to the lower levels
of creation where the *imago Dei* is least evident.
To speak of a new humanity is to anticipate an age
in which sexuality shares the unity of "man" as
imago Dei.

      While it may have been naive and senti-
mental for Americans to think of themselves as the
new Adam, it also prefigures a recognition of the
fact that humans live in separation from their
original intent--that the American saga is an
account that calls for the restoration of humanity.
Adam is Adam-Eve. The old humanity still lingers,
titillated by the barbarism of the shopping mall
culture. Therefore, we continue to use our sexuality as we used our axes and knives against the
"ice, the tiger, and the lion." Motorcycle manu-
facturers try to prolong the old humanity as they
appeal to our youth with ever more phallic designs
that thrust their bodies forth in elongated forms
that burst from the loins of reclining seats. We
are still amused and stimulated by the seductive
arts of the entertainment and commercial worlds.
But the end will be soon. The age must die. The
American saga has always carried the inexhaustible
symbol of the new humanity that promises an end to
artificial and arbitrary uses of man and woman.

      It was in the saga that women found a
means of telling a new story. Whether it was the
spirituality of Anne Hutchinson in 1636 or the more
extraordinary visions of Mother Ann Lee, there has
been present a "ready wit and bold spirit" that
defied the extensions of the old humanity. John
Winthrop called Hutchinson "that American Jezebel,"
but "women flocked to her home to hear her
comments." Mother Ann Lee may have seen herself as
the Bride of Christ, as the person of the Second
Advent, but there were those who sensed an
important dimension of a new truth. For her wisdom

was beyond her comprehension and the language of
the simple folk who heard her message. These women
are the "sectarians" in intellectual and religious
history. Like Mary Baker Eddy, they depart from
the main stream of acceptable rationality and
intellectual orthodoxy.

Here we are not concerned with the
integrity or credibility of their doctrines. What
they actually represent is the emergence of truth
that is not confined to the tight instrumentalities
of philosophical, scientific, and linguistic
"orthodoxies." And the coarse feminist ideologists
and crusaders of our own day are a demonstration of
the fact that we have not paid attention to the
wisdom expressed in such lives. The crusaders
began earlier than this century, of course, but
they are a vanguard of present-day frustration.
For ideologists and crusaders are always those who
are impatient and helpless in the midst of a revolution already occurring.

We get angry most frequently with those
injustices observed when a creative measure of
justice has already begun to assert itself. However, if we regard the American experience as a
matrix in which the birth of the new humanity is
forming, we will note that the *inevitable change
has been taking place*. It is the emergence of new
dimensions of truth and ways of understanding in
the life of persons such as Margaret Mead, Goergia
Harkness, and their forerunners in earlier
centuries that is true revolution and new birth.
For "consciousness" of the new humanity is something
to be *received*, to respond to, to participate in--
most often without attempting to reduce it to an
ideology. The new humanity is Adam-Eve, and it
will very likely be different in performance than
feminists demand, than behaviorists design, or
than technologists contrive in their test tubes.

III.

The new humanity is a new race. For a
time we may be reverting to tribalism and ethno-
centrism, but there is no stopping the emergence of

123

a new race, a new non-racial humanity. That process of emergence began in the earliest moments of the American saga, sometimes under the heartless ravishment of black women by the fathers and sons of White American plantations. But it began, nevertheless; and in some way that uniquely wanton form of conception is a reminder of the fact that the new humanity will come no matter how hard we cling to our absolute desires to preserve our own.

This is not to say that diversity and pluralism will no longer be part of the human scene. Racial and ethnic consciousness are wholesome ingredients in the unfolding drama. They provide identity and unity for peoples who must be able to bid for the power that is essential for full participation in the response to the American saga. We must remember that it was the intention of James Madison's governmental design to prevent individual and social interests from incorporating themselves too directly with the national political institution. Great diversity and pluralism would make it necessary for coalitions to form that represented the greatest common interest. Factions would be kept from imposing their passions on the rest of society. Nevertheless, multiplicity depended upon the ability of each group to assert itself in relation to some common goal. From this kind of coalition politics we learn that group identity and power are more important to the ongoing nature of our American experience than is any ideology. Andrew Greeley has written: "We will have effective racial integration and racial justice in the United States when the techniques and the policies designed to achieve such admirable social goals will bring clear benefit and profit not merely to blacks but to much of the rest of society." At the moment the Afro-American is understandably not so much concerned with "the rest of society" as he is with his own "benefit and profit;" and he is in process of acquiring the racial consciousness and political skill essential to full participation in the coalitions of power. However, what Greeley suggests may be "racial integration and racial justice" are an interlude in the saga. We must anticipate the physical regeneration

124

of a new race.

There is nothing in the American saga that will stop the narrative short of a new humanity which defies all previous ethnic and racial categories. The varieties are too great and too rich to escape the wonder of magnificent new physical and cultural conceptions. And, as a matter of fact, that is the only ultimate solution to racial crises. Once pride in racial and ethnic heritage is *really* achieved, it will no longer be a matter of defensive posturing or so-called "consciousness-raising." On university campuses, for example, the incidence of social intercourse between black and white is on the increase. Black consciousness is still important for purposes of security and identity, but it becomes decreasingly significant as the new generation finds itself honestly responding to human need and desire. Blacks and whites continue to be a threat to each other only so long as the ghetto mentality and reality exists in *absolute* separation from the coalitions of "the rest of society."

The ethnic factor has always asserted itself in the formation of the new humanity. From the very beginning of the American saga there has been intermarriage among the diversities of peoples who came from Europe. It was only when immigration occurred in ever-increasing numbers, with the dispossessed seeking both employment and the isolated identity of the ghetto, that ethnicity became a problem. Added to ethnicity itself, of course, was the formal religious factor. Decades of hostility between Catholic and Protestant made it difficult for creative relationship. But the ethnics very quickly learned the art of coalition politics fundamental to the American saga. And while defamatory salvos may continue to be fired across the streets that form the no-man's-land between the ethnic hollows, there has been regular and rapid escape from the warfare into relation-ships of skill, friendship, and marriage. Already in my own childhood the process had begun. My father was a coarse Pennsylvania German who was a laborer in the railroad years in the anthracite

125

regions of the state. He numbered among his
friends persons whom he constantly referred to as
"wop", "dago", and "Hunk" (probably only to be
called a "dumb Dutchman" in return). And the
intermarriage of those of diverse national origin
began among my friends and relatives. Archie
Bunker continued to refer to his son-in-law as a
crazy Polak, but the latter remained in Archie's
home as the potential father of his grandchildren.

IV.

        One of the unique dimensions of the new
racial character of the new humanity will be
pluralistic devotion. That is to say, in addition
to the physical regeneration that will gradually
dissipate the animosities of racial and ethnic
differences, there will arise a diversity of ways
of celebrating and reconstituting life's meaning.
What we have called religion will serve as traditional repositories of ultimate truth, providing
the many techniques, rituals, and theosophical
cultures necessary for human transformation and en-
richment. I have among my friends a young woman,
recently graduated from college. She is the child
of devout Roman Catholic heritage; and she herself
is a person who searches for the depth of understanding in her own tradition and what it may mean
in relation to other traditions. She is not a
rebel, but continues to be a faithful Roman Catholic. Her husband is Jewish, with what appears to
be a genuine appreciation of his own heritage.
The present traditional institutional characteristics of religion demand that the child born of
that union be baptized Roman Catholic. But that
kind of institutionalization of religious truth may
not be able to continue very long. For the physical regeneration of the emerging new humanity
already demands new institutional forms of religion.
The regeneration will increase, not decrease. The
Way of the Cross and the Torah will have to find
deeper traditional encounters of mutual nourishment
and the facillitation of pluralism in devotion
rather than mere institutional allegiance. Pluralism will continue, but we should not assume that it
will take the same form that we have inherited from

the past. After all, what was forced upon us by
the Greeks, the Muslims, the mystical revolution,
the sixteenth century reformations, and the
corporate models of industrial America, is hardly
sacred to the end of time. We must be open to
the kind of pluralism in religious truth that the
new humanity requires of us. What Joseph Washington tells us of the African traditional religions
must become true of us: "These religions were
dynamic, developed, and receptive to new religions."
James Cardinal Gibbons, in defense of the Knights
of Labor, said to Rome in 1887: "We believe...that
the circumstances of a people almost entirely
Catholic, as in lower Canada, must be very different from those of a mixed population like ours..."
It is that difference in circumstance that creates
in the American saga the necessity for a new
religious response to the new humanity.

V.

        The new humanity is also a political
creation. If coalition is that political art that
strives to bring together a diversity of interests
to the end that policies and programs will benefit
all of society, then it faces creative new possibilities. Labor will continue to be an interest
group that has legitimate demands for any coalition
to consider. It will not be necessary for labor to
agree to the utopian schemes and ideals of a
certain elite who wish to force their rhetoric on
all of society. Coalition is not concerned with
the success of ideals, only with the most effective
service to the people. Labor may lose some of its
ethnic and racial dimensions as the new humanity
emerges. Instead, the need to include labor in the
political design will be based on the fact that a
segment of the people in the saga perform a function
for the rest of society--a service that grants them
power to stand in the coalition. They are, therefore, not to be exploited by other interests.

        Scientific and technological interests
must likewise be forced into the necessities of
coalition politics. For too long a time they have
been relatively free agents, learning what they

127

wish to learn, devising what they wish to devise--
forcing the results of their efforts on the people.
Commercial, business, and industrial interests
build upon the absolutist work of technology, and
society has had little recourse but to acquiesce.
Whether the results of new discoveries and "products" are to the benefit of *all* the people is
seldom considered. The effects may be detrimental,
but that is something to be faced when the time
comes. Most of us have little voice in the
decisions made by scientific, commercial and
industrial interests. It is assumed that we are to
adjust to whatever great new discovery is made. We
are to be the recipients or the fictims of an elite
wisdom which we in our benighted condition cannot
comprehend. The automobile is in some sense the
paradigm here. If something is wrong with the
product, if it has some harmful effect on society,
the product is not corrected to the mutual economic
and social well-being of *all* the people. Rather, a
new product is produced. Except through the
agencies of government itself, many of us have no
access to the decisions that produce test-tube
babies and new cadillacs. Yet all of us are
affected, while the benefits to all are at least
dubious. The new humanity requires a more just and
effective way of promoting coalition politics.
Government must become less the management of the
schemes and self-interest of those involved in
leadership roles, and more the balancing of claims
to the common good.

        Perhaps no segment of our society is as
much in need of being required to respond to
coalition as the health professions. They exercise
an ever-greater autonomy and an increasing control
over the fate of humanity. The growing need for
human organs for transplant purposes gives rise to
a discussion of the question: when does death occur
and how is it determined, in order that organs may
be removed while still effective participants in
the life process? A medical professor, incensed
that anyone other than himself should be party to
such a decision, said in effect: "Only *I* can
determine what death is and when it is about to
occur!" That is an exceedingly dangerous and

totalitarian attitude. For it means that death is primarily a technological matter and that there is no knowledge or wisdom other than technical skill that contributes to the understanding of life, death, and human welfare. Medical, dental, and related professions must be made politically accountable. The decisions, practices, *and rewards* of the health professions are as much my concern as theirs, just as the fortunes of higher education are already very much influenced by those professions.

The coalitions essential to the politics of the new humanity require bold new shaping. The legal profession, sports, entertainment, and real estate development represent other areas exercising inordinate control over the society, without adequate channels for a coalition politics that is concerned with more equitable distribution of wealth, and policies that are to the benefit of *all* people.

It should be emphasized that I am speaking politically, not ideologically. I am not advocating ideals or utopian schemes. I am suggesting that the kind of political realism that has always been present in the American experience needs to be extended into the present. The American saga bears the symbol of a new humanity that demands a new style of realism. The old pluralism is giving way to a new one and we must be prepared to respond politically. The new humanity cannot function other than politically. It cannot have common ideals, but it can and does take place in a common narrative. The new humanity requires response in terms of the actualities of our existence. That makes us politicians in common cause, not crusaders or elite representatives of the truth. Our politics is one that enables decisional participation in the entire scale of human welfare. We have had considerable experience as participants in the support and direction of our educational enterprises. Only recently have we begun to give deference to a bureaucratic elite. That process must be reversed, and the principle of democratic decision extended to such common

concerns as medicine, technology, and commerce.
The saga beckons us toward a future in which the
drama of existence requires response to every
experience in which the power of meaning is encountered.

VI.

The new humanity is a common humanity.
When the earliest arrivals came to Penn's Woods
during the latter part of the seventeenth and the
early eighteenth centuries, they were a people who
saw as if for the first time. They witnessed that
world of "the lily," where the voice of the turtle
dove is heard, and they knew that all former human
distinctions had ceased to exist. It was to be a
land where persons were the aristocrats of their own
confession, where the leveller could follow the
dictates of his expectations. There is a dialectic
at work in the American saga, wherein levelling and
aristocratic tendencies are in constant tension,
bringing into being new versions of a common
humanity. Among the motivations of every leveller
is the desire to bring down the advantages of the
aristocrat to the level on which those advantages
are available to the leveller. The levelling impulse lives with an aristocratic dream. Each
successful levelling produces its aristocracy. Each
aristocracy experiences a gradual erosion of its
plantations. All aristocracies are to be short-
lived because it is a common humanity that comes
into being. For the black American it is necessary
that the white vision of the world be a place where
the peace includes the full enjoyment of the black
person. And so Joseph Washington asserts that "the
eradication of white folk religion is indispensable
because it is the undeniable demand of this historical era which can no longer be disregarded." Folk
religion that is tenaciously bound to its own perimeters must give way to a common humanity; it must
become a way of *all* the people.

This aspect of the image has implications
far beyond the confines of social class and racial
or ethnic concerns. I mean to say that the wisdom
of the people is trustworthy, that Andrew Jackson's

130

"Common Man" is to be the paradigm of the future.
But it is to be a common humanity far beyond the
imagination of the Jacksonian democrats, a community that brings into dialogue the richness of
the lore of great diversities of peoples.   I
emphasize that it is a commonality of wisdom.   I
recall an incident during those days when, in the
academic and theological worlds, we had begun to be
enamored of the need for "community." Theologians
wrote of the church as the "community of faith,"
and we were admonished to help make manifest the
"community" dimension of existence. I had a
friend at the time, who was a professor at a small
liberal arts college. One day he said to me, "You
know, I find more community down at the local auto
repair shop than I do in the church." What he
obviously meant was that there was a greater
honesty, openness of encounter, and less pretense
than the church ordinarily presents.   In many ways,
churches have become assemblies of pretenders, who
suffer the surprise of controversy and antagonism
in the context of committee meetings. They just
can't imagine anyone talking like that, acting like
that--*in church!* But where there is less pretense,
there is more community.

        Community is a manifestation of what
humans have in common. This in no way implies that
everything is in common. There is great inequality
of talent, opportunity, and intelligence. But the
wisdom of understanding and accepting the commonality of the human situation is available to all.
Frequently, the inherited and invented maxims of
the seemingly uneducated are an expression of that
wisdom. Sometime ago an issue of Ebony hailed the
"primitive" or "naive" art of Elijah Pierce,
octogenarian barber from Columbus, Ohio, whose
brightly colored carvings have been on exhibit in
many of the world's galleries. Elijah was
"discovered" when he was 79 years old. "Critics
were impressed with what one of them has described
as the 'natural sense of abstraction and design' in
his carvings," said Ebony. The young sculptor who
has helped to promote Pierce's work adds, "I was
overwhelmed by the honesty and simplicity of his
work. You see many lies in art hanging on walls in

131

galleries and museums. His work is the real thing,
like the man himself."

          The wisdom of the common man is in his
honesty and simplicity. The implication is that
the greater the self-consciousness of training and
education, the less the presence of honesty and
simplicity. To the degree that that is so, we face
a considerable dilemma today. We can expect a
decrease in wisdom and an increase of the "lies"
that hang in the museums and galleries of postcivilization. Too many elites in the realms of
education, medicine, and art become separated from
what they have in common with the rest of humanity.
They lack wisdom and become the practitioners of
superficiality and pretense. Hopefully we shall
still be able to discover that we are not of our
own contrivance, that our apparent knowledge is
not the measure of our personhood. The fact that
artistry can come from the untrained, that helpful
skills and knowledge can be derived from the "uneducated," is a testimony to our common humanity.
The teaching of the Humanities in the colleges and
universities is slowly recognizing the parochialism
of its pretense. It has been traditionally assumed
that the only worthwhile humanizing expressions
have been canonically established in the heritage
of Plato, Bach, Rubens, and Dante. Gradually we
have begun to understand that we have been ignoring
the wisdom, the humanizing work, of millions who
were never aware of the principals in the academic
pantheon. When we take a new and humble look at
folk art and lore, the mythology, magic, and
religion of "the people," we shall be on the way
to advancing the power of meaning in the symbol of
the new humanity.

          Wisdom is not the possession of an elite,
certainly not of an educated elite. Today's formal
education has become a form of initiation into the
function of society. At its best it deepens our
understanding of the knowledge we acquire. It is
not a means of salvation, hardly a guarantee of
wisdom. Wisdom emerges from the honesty of our
sensibility to the common human condition. We must
be appreciative of the fact that there is probably

more truth, artistry, and wisdom in the hills of
Tennessee and in the Jewish ghetto than in the de-
partment of philosophy.

During the famous debates between
Stephen A. Douglas and Abraham Lincoln in 1854,
the latter drew from the depth of his spiritual
resources in order to demonstrate the frivolity of
Douglas' views on slavery. Those depths were
marked by the wisdom of his common humanity, a
wisdom that was greater than the learning he had
undertaken. William Wolf tells us that Lincoln
went deeper than "self-evidence" for his understanding of the implications of the Declaration of
Independence. "Slavery is founded in the selfish-
ness of human nature," said Lincoln. "Repeal the
Missouri Compromise...repeal all past history, you
still cannot repeal human nature. It still will be
the abundance of man's heart, that slavery extension is wrong." The abundance of man's heart is a
feature of the new humanity of the American saga.
The abundance of man's heart is the fullness toward
which we move, seizing upon "the farthest posterity."

Reflect for a moment upon your deepest
understanding and yearning. Is it not true that
the symbol of the new humanity is basic to your
appraisal of the future of our existence? We live
by the power it shares with us, suggesting the
beauty of a new race; and we are keenly aware of
the sharp necessity of the political moments that
require new coalitions of participation. Living as
we do, between the times, we cannot describe the
full portrait of our common humanity, but we know
we can neither think nor act without the symbol.
"As for the cities we have," writes Paol Soleri,
"we will live with them. We cannot live for them.
Thus, while effort will go into improving what we
have, great and persistent effort must go into the
development, parallel to the condemned patterns, of
new systems coherent with man's needs." Soleri's
arcology and Elijah Pierce's primitive carvings--
they are the witness of a presence in the American
saga--a presence of wisdom from the image of a new
humanity that rises up even as decay and meaninglessness smother us in the rubble of all that is old.

133

134

CHAPTER VIII

THE WONDER WORKING OF PROVIDENCE

Some years ago I was immersed in the oppressive waters of that murky ocean common to all professorial voyages--the ofttimes dismal depths of doctoral dissertation. I must admit that much of the research was rather fascinating. I was investigating the influence of nineteenth century Evangelical Portestantism on the beginnings of land-grant education. And so I examined the documents of agricultural and educational societies, early catalog copies, and presidential reports and addresses. One word stood out from amid the rhetoric of public higher education in the nineteenth century. It is the word "Providence." I have concluded that the term is at least as important as what has been called "manifest destiny." And although the two words may be inextricably related in the actualities of the last century, they are separate terms; and, in fact, the image of Providence is more prevalent than the doctrine of manifest destiny. The belief in manifest destiny was quite frequently a distortion of the power of meaning resident in the image of Providence.

To the designers of democratic higher education--in land-grant colleges and state universities--the image of Providence was a prominent vehicle of understanding and purpose. To them America had to fashion new models of education because the very course of history offered a stirring mandate. The future of the nation demanded that a new kind of education be developed, one that would be available to all classes of people, one that would prepare them for the kinds of work that needed doing as the new century approached. Only a wise and wonder-working Providence could explain the great potential of America in such circumstance. Only the fire at night and the cloud by day was adequate to a task of such proportions. And in speech after speech, report after report, there appeared the thanksgivings of leaders, alongside that peculiar prophetic note of the Puritan strain

135

of American consciousness, the jeremiad. For there had always been present the thought that we must measure up, that failure to do so might bring the agony of defeat rather than the assurance of triumph. "Take note of the Providence that has produced such greatness!" they exclaimed. "Take heed that you may be worthy; be honorable in your dedication and pursuit!" they admonished.

I have asked myself, what figures, what visible realities accompanied the thought of Providence. "...though I thought not of thee under the form of a human body, yet I was constrained to image Thee to be something corporeal in space, either infused into the world, or infinitely diffused beyond it...since whatsoever I conceived, deprived of this space, appeared as nothing to me, yea, altogether nothing, not even a void..." So St. Augustine in his Confessions. It is somewhat comforting to learn that there is absolutely no way to escape associating our most refined conceptual thought with some kind of visible imagery. I recall a period in my thinking when I was a bit enamoured of *elan vital* as a most satisfactory way of conceiving the life process which served as a sufficient point of departure for a doctrine of God. It was quite disconcerting to discover that I had been thinking of something quite tangible, of a sort of "running on" of a thick gooey substance, rather like endless rubber cement.

I must confess that Providence, like *elan vital*, has some visual accompaniment for me. I think first of a mysterious table set in the midst of a beautiful and thick great forest. And on that table there is a kind of mound of bright red apples and golden oranges. Grapes in blue and purple and silver-green jackets cascade among melons and pumpkins, squash and plums. But I can't really see *all* that is there, and if I were to go on describing the ingredients in detail, I would be making arbitrary and artificial decision. For I envision colors and ripeness that blend their shapes into the mystery of a fuller image. What does it mean that I have conjured up that picture from somewhere among the associations of my conceptual thinking?

136

Certainly one possible reply is that Providence
points to the mystery of the way in which we are
provided for.

What else lingers in my bank of images?
There is one that I am somewhat ashamed to reveal.
For I thought I had expelled it by the rigors of
philosophical and theological analysis. I remember laughing at those who used this image as if
they meant it literally. There is a hand. Sometimes it points, sometimes it holds. Although it
points mostly ahead of me, it also points to the
rear. I know for certain *there is no hand;* but I
can't expel the figure of it. And I can't bring
myself to sing that song that has become a main-
stay of avant-garde corporate worship: "He's got
the whole world in his hands!" Somehow that seems
to cheapen the image of the hand. So why do I
retain the image? Because the hand is the mysterious agency of approach and of intimacy. The hand
works at the fashioning of human sustenance and
beauty. The hand guides and suggests direction;
it reassures us by pointing to the rear--assures
us that the way we have come was not without
purpose or meaning. The hand greets, it gestures.
It holds a child and caresses a lover. How could
I *possibly* escape the image of the hand when I
think--however abstractly--of Providence? For that
matter, whether the symbol of Providence is
prominent in my mind or not, can I do without the
transcendent significance of the hand? Perhaps
only if I cease to be human.

There is a risk, I suppose, that lies
before those who are sensible to the image of
Providence. There is the image of the question
mark, a No as well as a Yes to all that has been
and is to come. Providence is not some petty
assurance that "all will be well." It is not the
bedside deception in the face of terminal illness,
not the sanguine promise that the raging storm will
not ravage our hearth. No Puritan father, no salty
Calvinist ever assumed that Providence was the
promise of a fully paid vacation trip to the exotic
gardens of the emerald forest. Providence stands
like the great lion, between us and the stream of

water that nourishes our existence. We must decide
whether we have the courage to drink. Providence
provides, it offers, it sustains; but somehow,
under that same image is an awareness of the fact
that the *real* blessings of existence are not fully
known by us. Our own self-centered projections
and demands produce an unreal ingredient in every
investment of time and effort. When we equate
these fictions with Providence itself, we make it
necessary for the "No" and the question mark. The
American saga carries in its continuum an image of
Providence that permits no naive cult of "positive
thinking" even among the spokesmen for its powerful
symbols.

I.

I suppose I could conjure up more of the
tangible images that accompany my understanding of
Providence. But perhaps it would begin to be too
contrived an artistry. My suspicion is that there
is no American who does not live with similar
images, no participant in the saga who escapes the
meaning of Providence. And if there are those who
have rejected the name because their sophistication
rejects all such concrete allusions to a transcendent meaning, they must be reminded that their
most refined thinking is beleaguered with substan-
tive images that have not nearly so great a perfection as what they reject.

If Providence is appositional to the
story of our very identity and purpose as a people,
it may help us to explore some of its implications.
Yet anything we say in more analytical or descrip-
tive fashion will relate to those reflections we
have just finished. First, the symbol of Providence retains and bestows the character of wonder.
The authentic life is, as G. K. Chesterton said,
being "happy in this wonderland without once being
merely comfortable." Traditional humanity of the
primal, Greek, and Judeo-Christian patterns of
Western history lived in a "wonder-ful" cosmos,
says Sam Keen in Apology for Wonder. Wonder is
usually associated with the Dionysian rather than
the Apollonian way, continues Keen; and even

138

Christianity came onto the scene as a Dionysian
protest "against the stifling domination of Apollo."
Of course, the authentic life is one of timeliness
and balance, but the important admonition for
modern humanity is that we rediscover the wonder
we have lost as *homo faber* or *homo fabricatus*.

Children are still capable of living in
a wonder-ful world, but I suspect even that potential is decreasing. There is nothing wonder-ful
about those mechanical little show business person-
alities, created by the geniuses of electronic
commercialism. They are the humunculi of *homo
faber*--queer little people who titillate our techno-
cratized sensitivities with their contrived
maturity and manipulated humor. Of course, these
commercially fabricated youngsters are in a
minority, but they are increasing in number. And
there is some evidence to suggest that the average
child is less and less open to the possibilities of
wonder.

From the days when the black-robed
Jesuits struggled in the harsh borderlands of the
Southwest to those ecstatic moments when Lewis and
Clark found themselves on the vaulted green bank of
a shimmering new river, there has been wonder to
the American saga. The red man rode slowly through
the red rocks of the pine-scented canyon, chanting
and knowing that all was well. Providence
symbolizes the power of the More Than in life to
offer itself, to become something *for us*, perhaps
to us, with us.

Edward Johnson looked on the "first
planting" of his people in the New England of the
seventeenth century, contrasted it with "the sad
condition of England, when this people removed," then
said: "Lord Christ, here they are at they command,
they go, this is the door thou hast opened upon
our earnest request, and we hope it shall never be
shut: for Englands sake they are going from
England to pray without ceasing for England, O
England! thou shalt find New England prayers pre-
vailing with their God for thee..." How wonder-
ful, said Johnson, that huts were provided,

139

"dwellings in the Desert Wilderness," that the land
purchased from Indians yielded to the perseverence
of these people, that the increase of the Church
should take place against the clamor of Babylon and
Antichrist. How amazing that two of New England's
most valiant leaders should have been saved from
English conspiracy and delivered safely to America!
"But the Lord Christ--intending to make his New
England Souldiers the very wonder of this Age,
brought them into greater straites, that this
Wonder working Providence might the more appear in
their deliverance..." (italics mine)

This is not an apology for New England--
only for the wonder working of Providence. Today
we read such accounts with understandable skepti-
cism and critical judgment. But what we overlook
is that the loss of the sensibility to Providence
has brought with it the absence of wonder. It is
not for us to say finally whether Edward Johnson
was right or wrong in his self-righteous ecstasy.
To do so is to make some clever claim that protects
us against the surprise, the shock of wonder itself.
Providence relates only to the actual substance and
condition of humanity at any one time and place.
Providence relates to the wonder of this moment,
around this corner, through this pressure of pain.

Providence is the understanding of
events as part of a wonder-ful story. It places
the successes and failures of life in a perspective
that permits reflection upon the *meaning* of
experience and events. The wonder of existence
comes from knowing that somehow all is provided
for in the story we are living. Providence helps
us to know that reality is More Than the routine
we commonly accept, and that the routine can be
accepted because it may be transformed.

In Frank Waters' novel of a Pueblo Indian,
The Man Who Killed the Deer, young Martiniano has
spoken to a girl from far away, whom he wishes to
have as his wife. It had been a very "undignified
American" way of going about things--speaking to
the girl in this way, without deference to tribal
custom. His friends could not believe that any-

140

thing good could come of his arrangements. Martiniano was an outcast because of behavior inappropriate to the Indian ways. He had seen the girl but once, and he was poor and without standing. Did he really expect her to return to him? "There was that within him which spoke with faith. It is a strange thing, this. All they say is true. But it is the little truth which does not matter. It is the big truth that fills me. Who can say the words that belong to it?" There it is--the power of the big truth, that which allows wonder and possibility to exist in the face of all odds to the contrary! And even if Martiniano was an outcast, corrupted by the ways of the white man, his corruptibility could not eliminate the ubiquitous character of wondering possibility that is part of our humanity. One way or another, the saga will bring its tales, its big truth to us so that we may wonder. And the wonder itself is a signification from the symbol of Providence--that good shall come, that not even privation and death can remove the power of meaning that is our eternal possibility.

II.

The symbol of Providence is a bearer of the presence of creation. Providence reminds us that what is is created, that we may not have *final* answers about the when and how of what *is*; but that there is *present* to us in our experience a sensibility to the fact that we are *participants* in what is, and that that need not be the case. The effort of every true artist is an agonized attempt to portray that fact, even in the face of every evidence to the contrary. When the artist creates he participates in either a celebratory or rebellious demonstration that the More Than is the truest feature of existence.

What has been is created, it did not simply occur. For if the latter were the case, we should be unable to contribute anything either to its facticity or to its potential. We, too, would be part of that simple facticity. So while the creation is experienced by us as a continuing pro-

141

cess, it is a mere witness to us concerning the
character of what is. Providence makes present to
us the reality of creation. The manner of that
"making present" is experienced as a process.
Providence has been an important symbol in the
American saga in the sense that our entire history
is based on the precarious manner in which we
continue to build our existence at the edges of
threatening wildernesses, or on the slopes overlooking almost magical portraits of verdant
pastures and snug forests.

There has always been present to our
experience some evidence of the fact that what is
need not be. We have been tempted by a False
Provider as well as guided by Providence. We have
been a people of haste and greed because the table
set before us was like a mysterious banquet
secretly placed in a hidden corner of a forest
inhabited by vagabonds. The question facing the
finder is whether to devour it all in a hurry, or
to inform the rest of the brotherhood. The childhood game of "finders keepers, losers weepers" has
been very much present with us. It is the dogma
of the False Provider who wants us to assume that
our superior fate, our craft, is the source of
goodness. It is an attitude that rejects the
givenness of creation and its goodness, refuses to
see the provisional character of existence. It is
the neglect of the power of Providence and the
substitution of grim determination for the artful-
ness of gratitude.

What the American continent and its great
spaces represented was really *too good to be true*.
And the curious combination of space and of un-
determined policy and control--these, too, made
for possibilities *too good to be true*. It was all
a miracle--even the desert wastes and the mon-
otonous plains. It was a magic wonderland like no
visitor had ever seen before. It was, it is; it
need not be; tomorrow it *might not* be. The truth
of it all lay before us, but it was so unlike the
ordinary expectations of human history that we
hastily moved to claim it, to capture the magic
out of the feat that we might lose it.

142

We have frequently forgotten the creation
that lies before us and within us. Instead we
assumed that all that opened before us as possibility was ours to possess. Providence was no
longer a witness to creation but the stamp of our
own self-approval. The eventual result of such
thinking is the disappearance of the symbol from
meaningful use. If Providence is merely the mark
of approval for every human claim, then we
eventually devise an ethic that is no ethic at
all--rather it is simple prudential catering to our
whims and aims. Providence itself finally becomes
a matter of archaic vocabulary.

Nevertheless, it becomes abundantly
clear in the perspective of history itself that the
power of meaning in the symbol will assert itself.
If it has been the bearer of significant meaning,
reflective of the appositional character of life,
then the symbol and its meaning are not finally
lost. Either there is creation or there is not.
And if we forget it, or ignore it; if the symbol
of Providence has ceased to confirm and help us
care for creation, then distortion will be the
result and catastrophe the end. For the chaos
over which creation has established its sacred
victory makes existence extremely precarious. If
we forget the sacredness, the chaos will return,
and all of the contrivances of human technology
will accomplish nothing but illusion.

Rebbe Nahman of Bratzlav, one of Elie
Wiesel's "souls on fire" once told this tale:
"Once upon a time there was a country that
encompassed all the countries of the world. And
in that country, there was a town that incorpor-
ated all the towns of the country; and in that
town there was a street in which were gathered all
the streets of the town; and on that street was a
house that sheltered all the houses of the street;
and in that house was a room, and in that room
there was a man, and that man personified all men
of all countries and that man laughed and laughed
--no one had ever laughed like that before." To
me that man is the participant in the American
saga who understands Providence; and who watches

each town, each street and house, each person pretending to be the explicit master of its own fate--
unable to see the creation in which it lives.

IV.

Providence is a symbol of the fact that
we are both nature and More Than nature. Reinhold
Niebuhr went to great pains in his Gifford
Lectures on The Nature and Destiny of Man to bring
some clarity to the truth that humanity belongs "to
the realm of nature *and* to the realm of spirit."
The magic of participation in creation is
tempered by the fact that we are expected to share
responsibility for the course of things. We live
in anxiety, says Niebuhr, because there is an
apparent limitation and dependence to our lives,
yet we are not so limited that we are not *aware* of
our limitations. The truth of this insight may be
observed the world over. When the Bodhisattva ideal
makes its way into Buddhist thought and style, there
has entered the notion that it is possible for enlightenment and liberation to take place *in relation
to the actualities* of existence. The Bodhisattva
is the one who sacrifices what might appear to be
his own perfection in order that there might occur
a deeper oneness with others and a greater power to
serve them. This development represents, in a very
significant manner, a coming to terms with historical reality. While the Theravada teacher may reject such doctrine, and the interpreter of Mahayana
may wish to point out that it is the *real* meaning
of original Buddhist teaching, the development itself *is a development*. And it is an acknowlegment
of the fact that limitations can only be served,
not entirely surmounted. The ideal becomes one of
a relational perfection rather than an absolute
perfection which denies part of the truth of human
existence. The Bodhisattva ideal is a real nexus
for dialogue between Far Eastern thought and the
Judeao-Christian traditions.

I have made reference to Buddhist development here not only because it illustrates in its
own way what Niebuhr and many other Western thinkers have made profound efforts to explain, but also

144

because, as Buddhist ways become more fully part of
the American saga they will find themselves in
creative contact with the symbol of Providence itself.

Providence means that the destiny of
humanity is worked out in constant creative tension
between the realm of nature and the realm of spirit.
Spirit represents our transcendence of the nature
in which we participate. Our spirituality is the
cause of the anxiety which Niebuhr describes.
Spirituality is evidence of the tension between
limitation and possibility. It is the freedom
derived of spirit that makes for responsibility and
accounts for the unpredictability of events. And
it is the limitation enforced by nature that makes
responsibility possible and events inevitable. The
results are what is called history. Providence is
the symbol assuring us that even in our responsibility, everything does not depend upon us--that the
worst conditions of history retain provisions of
goodness and meaning.

This is no deterministic posture--it is
not to say, whatever will be will be. It is not
the belief in some divine decreee established in
mechanical and arbitrary fashion before the worlds
began. It is not the placing of the pins in some
charted map of divine corporation strategy. As
Paul Tillich has pointed out, Providence is the
evidence of "...directing creativity (working)
through the spontaneity of creatures and human
freedom...It is misleading to speak of a divine
'design,' even if it is not understood in a
deterministic way. For the term 'design' has the
connotation of a preconceived pattern, including
all the particulars which constitute a design."

The forces and experiences of destruction, corruption, evil and disintegration do not
disappear; they are not obliterated, but they
cannot prevent Providence from its continuing
creational witness. For the purposes and aims that
have been activated out of the darkness before
historical history cannot be finally thwarted. The
power of meaning that is appositionally shared with

145

us is a promise of greater abundance that is to be.
It is rather like C. S. Lewis' story of The Lion,
the Witch, and the Wardrobe. Once the children saw
Aslan, the great lion, they somehow knew something
inexplicable, but unforgettable, unchangeable. They
had had no idea who he was, but even at the mention
of his name "each one of the children felt something
jump in his inside." From that moment on, seeing
Aslan or not seeing him, the world was changed.
There was a presence in it and outside it, in sight
or in expectation. The children knew that they and
the world were somehow provided for. They had a
truth for understanding existence that held before
them the vision of fulfillment.

Providence is provision for the actualities and potentialities of existence, but it is
also provisional. We are provided for; there is a
More Than that constantly offers itself to the
total well-being of our lives. But we are
never in a position to know precisely what the end
will be; nor are we to assume that being provided
for is the assurance that we can rest in the realm
of nature, content that "things will turn out all
right." For we must remember that Providence is a
reference from the realm of spirit as well as of
nature--assuring us only that there is a freedom
about the whole of existence which is unpredictable.

"We have been the recipients of the
choicest bounties of Heaven" said Abraham Lincoln.
"We have been preserved, these many years, in
peace and prosperity. We have grown in numbers,
wealth and power, as no other nation has ever grown.
But we have forgotten...the gracious hand which
has preserved us in peace, and multiplied and enriched and strengthened us; and we have vainly
imagined, in the deceitfulness of our hearts that
all these blessings were produced by some superior
wisdom and virtue of our own." This was the same
narrator of the American saga who was able to
discern the foolhardiness of those who dared to
assume "Tod is on our side." For Lincoln
understood Providence as that power which tends
toward unity and gratitude, which provides, but
cannot be taken for granted. Lincoln knew that the

146

American experience was a grand story, a saga to be
lived responsively by "an almost chosen people."
"It is not the story itself, but its purpose and
effect that interests me...No, I am not simply a
storyteller," he said, "but storytelling as an
emollient saves me friction and distress."

V.

There is a kind of retrospect to our
ability to respond to the symbol of Providence.
Among some of the first immigrants to come to
Penn's Woods were Mennonites from South Germany.
One such pioneer received a letter from his father
in Heilbron as early as 1681. "America, according
to your writing," said the father, "must be a
beautiful land. We rejoice greatly that your home
is with such God-fearing people, and that the
Indians in your community are a peace-loving people."
He goes on to write about the worsening of conditions in South Germany and of a visit from a
merchant who spoke of a new group of Rhinelanders
about to leave for the "New World." "When I gave
the good man your letter to read, he was greatly
surprised, and said that you were in the land to
which these emigrants are going. It is the good
providence of God that has shown these burdened
people so glorious a land. We, as also the Platten-
bach family, are only waiting for a good opportunity
when the dear Lord will bring us to you." The
father reflects upon the coincidence of events--he
looks back and comes to the *conclusion* that "it is
the good providence of God."

Only by glimpsing the entire landscape,
as far as the eye of faith can see, will we begin
to understand that what is and what is to be are in
terms of Providence. I see something of this in the
American genre and landscape painters of the 19th
century. Of course, many of them were influenced
by the art schools and colonies of Europe. They
had succumbed to the schizoid pressure of American
culture, gone abroad to gain depth from the older
and more refined cultures of the Old World. A
painting like Washington Allston's "Moonlit Landscape" may reflect the ennui of Europe, or even a
sense of the relentless power of nature and its

147

inevitable triumph over humankind. But somehow the painting reflects a wider landscape, derived of experience of the American saga. As a result, there is a sense of Providence that reassures. We are aware of the fact that there is a hope that will not be denied. It looks at the events of an immediate past from the retrospective vantage point of ongoing creation.

The hackneyed and worshipful chant, "You can't stop Progress," rings in our ears, lingers over the dead bodies of the displaced animals and ravaged flesh of Southeast Asia, and moans along the parched cobbles of dried-up river beds. It is an abstract cry, a meaningless creed. There is no substance to it--only blind and self-centered belief. Progress is matter of belief, response to the half-truth in the dialectic of the symbol of Providence. Providence always beckons us onward and reassures us of the meaning of events in retrospect. It says 'no,' however, to any attempt to limit its goodness to our desires.

Kevin Starr, reflecting on the "California Dream," points out the failure of many clergy to be the proponents of the fullness of Providence during the development of California. They were "too ready to equate each event with the Lord's purposes." They identified Progress with Providence and lost "an independent basis for understanding, the sort of consciousness and moral stance appropriate to religious witness, in and of the world, yet secretly and strangely free." There is a sobriety to a full understanding of Providence, derived of the fact that we are more graciously aware of it as we "look back." When we have been surprised in this manner by its presence in *what has occurred*, we take heart for the future. But we are sober because we shall only know the truth of Providence when we again "look back." All power of meaning is encountered at the horizons of our existence; and the horizon that seems to us the edge of the future rejects any attempt to enclose it. We are only aware of the extent of its offering to us when we look back on that terrain that has become our past horizon.

148

We cannot truly live without the symbol of Providence. We can subsist, we can become help-less figures in a deathful collage that is no longer a saga; but we live behind an uncanny wall. Like the cinder blocks that encircle the compressed yards of the post-civilization in the Arizona desert, there is no transparency. I gaze and I can only try to imagine--perhaps remember--what lies on the other side. I recall the response of our aging collie, Tammy, to this experience for the first time. She had been accustomed to a rather large back yard in Pennsylvania. There we had limited her wanderings somewhat, but not her visibility, by erecting a wire field fence around that quadrangle. It was possible for her to see anything going on beyond those confines. The ex-perience of the courtyard wall of Arizona was an extremely anxious and frustrating one for her. She ran along the baffling edges of that barrier, some-times feverishly. She knew there was something beyond it. She could smell and she could recall, but there was no way for images to break through. And then she died.

The symbol of Providence provides, pre-serves, and protects. But it is also transparent to what lies beyond. Separating the chancel and nave of Orthodox churches is the icon wall, covered with the stylized images that receive the reverent kisses of the worshipper. The icons are a transparency between earthly and celestial worlds. Each world beholds the other through the icono-stasis (icon wall); and "the church itself is an icon of heaven," says Ernst Benz, "while man ("in the *image* of God") carries the icon of God within himself." An appreciative awareness of what that represents opens us to the vision of Providence as we become the storytellers, the pilgrim narrators of the American saga.

AFTERWORD

The reader has discovered that this book has been influenced by a great variety of authors. Quotations and ideas have been used, not to engage in scholarly intrigue, but to reveal the manner in which I have become host to thoughts which I believe are universal. In order for thoughts to be universal, they need not bow to the canons of a single consistent system or structure; they need only find incarnation in a person and among people. I have avoided footnotes and end notes so that the reader may deal primarily with my particular embodiment of ideas. However, some of the works that have influenced my thinking and served as the source of quotation are offered here. Many will already be well known to the reader.

Beaver, R. Pierce. Church, State, and American Indians. St. Louis: Concordia Publishing House, 1966.

Bellah, Robert N. The Broken Covenant. New York: Seabury Press, 1975.

Chase, Richard. Grandfather's Tales. Boston: Houghton Mifflin Co., 1948.

Dillenberger, John. Countours of Faith. Nashville: Abingdon Press, 1967.

Eiseley, Loren. The Immense Journey. New York: Vintage Books, 1959.

_____. The Invisible Pyramid. New York: Charles Scribner's Sons, 1970.

Eliade, Mircea. The Sacred and the Profane. New York: Harcourt, Brace and World, Inc., 1959.

Ellul, Jacques. Hope in Time of Abandonment. New York: The Seabury Press, 1973.

Greeley, Andrew M. Building Coalitions: American
    Politics in the 1970s. New York: New Viewpoints,
    1974.

Handy, Robert T. A Christian America. New York:
    Oxford University Press, 1971.

James, Joseph. The Way of Mysticism. London:
    Jonathan Cape, 1950.

Jones, Rufus M. Studies in Mystical Religion. London:
    Macmillan, 1932, 1972.

Lewis, C. S. The Chronicles of Narnia. Vols. I,
    II. New York: Religious Book Club, 1972.

Lewis, R. W. B. American Adam. Chicago: Uni-
    versity of Chicago Press, 1955, 1972.

Lippmann, Walter. A Preface to Morals. New York:
    The Macmillan Company, 1929.

Marty, Martin E. A Nation of Behavers. Chicago:
    University of Chicago Press, 1976.

Marx, Leo. The Machine in the Garden. New York:
    Oxford University Press, 1967, 1972.

Mead, Sidney E. The Lively Experiment. New York:
    Harper and Row, 1963.

_____. The Nation with the Soul of a Church.
    New York: Harper and Row, 1975.

Michaelsen, Robert S. The American Search for
    Soul. Baton Rouge: Louisiana State University
    Press, 1975.

Needleman, Jacob. The New Religions. Garden City,
    New York: Doubleday and Co., Inc., 1970.

_____. A Sense of the Cosmos. Garden City,
    New York: Doubleday and Co., Inc., 1975.

Niebuhr, Reinhold. The Nature and Destiny of Man. New York: Charles Scribner's Sons, Inc., 1949.

Novak, Michael. Ascent of the Mountain, Flight of the Dove. New York: Harper and Row, 1971.

_____. Choosing Our King. New York: Macmillan Publishing Co., Inc., 1974.

Richardson, Herbert W. Toward an American Theology. New York: Harper and Row, 1967.

Richey, Russell E. and Jones, Donald G., eds. American Civil Religion. New York: Harper and Row, 1974.

Sandburg, Carl. Harvest Poems 1910-1960. New York: Harcourt, Brace and World, Inc., 1960.

_____. Honey and Salt. New York: Harcourt, Brace and World, Inc., 1963.

Shah, Indries. The Sufis. Garden City, New York: Doubleday and Co., Inc., 1971.

Slotkin, Richard. Regeneration Through Violence. Middletown, Connecticut: Wesleyan University Press, 1973.

Smith, Henry Nash. Virgin Land. Cambridge, Massachusetts: Harvard University Press, 1971.

Smith, Huston. Forgotten Truth. New York: Harper and Row, 1976.

Starr, Kevin. Americans and the California Dream. New York: Oxford University Press, 1973.

Thompson, William I. At the Edge of History. New York: Harper and Row, 1971.

Tillich, Paul. Christianity and the Encounter of World Religions. New York: Columbia University Press, 1963.

_____. Systematic Theology. Vol. III. Chicago: University of Chicago Press, 1963, 1966.

Tuveson, Ernest Lee. Redeemer Nation. Chicago: University of Chicago Press, 1968.

Waters, Frank. Book of the Hopi. New York: Ballantine Books, 1963, 1972.

_____. The Man Who Killed the Deer. New York: Pocket Books, 1972.

Wiesel, Elie. Souls on Fire. New York: Vintage Books, 1973.

Wolf, William. The Religion of Abraham Lincoln. New York: Seabury Press, 1963.

About the Author

Richard E. Wentz is Professor of Religious Studies at Arizona State University, Tempe, Arizona, where he teaches courses in American religion and in Religion and Story. He has published essays in theology, folk religion, and regionalism in American religion. Professor Wentz formerly taught at The Pennsylvania State University and the Mercersburg Academy.

DATE DUE

GAYLORD | | | PRINTED IN U.S.A.